Did You Kill Anyone?

Reunderstanding My Military
Experience as a Critique of
Modern Culture

Did You Kill Anyone?

Reunderstanding My Military
Experience as a Critique of
Modern Culture

Scott Beauchamp

Winchester, UK
Washington, USA

JOHN HUNT PUBLISHING

First published by Zero Books, 2020
Zero Books is an imprint of John Hunt Publishing Ltd., No. 3 East St., Alresford,
Hampshire SO24 9EE, UK
office@jhpbooks.com
www.johnhuntpublishing.com
www.zero-books.net

For distributor details and how to order please visit the 'Ordering' section on our website.

Text copyright: Scott Beauchamp 2018

ISBN: 978 1 78535 786 2
978 1 78535 787 9 (ebook)
Library of Congress Control Number: 2018961974

A CIP catalogue record for this book is available from the British Library.

Design: Stuart Davies

UK: Printed and bound by CPI Group (UK) Ltd, Croydon, CR0 4YY
US: Printed and bound by Thomson-Shore, 7300 West Joy Road, Dexter, MI 48130

We operate a distinctive and ethical publishing philosophy in
all areas of our business, from our global network of authors to
production and worldwide distribution.

Contents

Chapter 1: Boredom   1

Chapter 2: Ritual   19

Chapter 3: Community   38

Chapter 4: Hierarchy   58

Chapter 5: Smoking   77

Chapter 6: Tradition   92

Chapter 7: Honor   112

Postscript   125

Acknowledgments   127

Bibliography   128

Biography   133

For Nika

Chapter 1

Boredom

I knew there would be questions after the war.

"Did you kill anyone?"

I was ready for that one, the biggest and most intimidating. That question would hang as an ominous backdrop to nearly every conversation about my time in Iraq, and especially prominent in the ones in which I could sense the subject being meticulously avoided. I anticipated the question because it was always there no matter what we were actually talking about.

How I answered depended on who was asking and how they put the question to me. An informal decision tree, intuitive and complex, coalesced in my mind. If the kid asking was bleary-eyed and smiling, swaying drunk on a porch outside of a party, I would demure.

"Oh, don't worry about it man. I'm just trying to enjoy the party."

Never be eager to indulge the fantasies of young civilians hungry for the illusion of second-hand honor. They don't actually gain anything and you feel vulgar afterwards. Save the vulgarity for the brothers you served with where, rooted in shared experience, gallows humor reaffirms and exalts your bond.

"We don't have to talk about it if you don't want to, but did you kill anyone?"

The question might come from someone who feels obligated to help guide you through your experiences. Their intentions are most likely only superficially magnanimous. They have no idea what they're talking about. Therapy offered so casually is just as presumptuous and shallow as trying to force the personal experience of combat into drunken party conversation.

"I don't think I'm ready to talk about that yet..."

The only kind of warrior that people offering therapy understand is a wounded one. You can throw them off of your trail by doubling down on the identity they've assigned you. Their assumptions can become your escape hatch.

Then there are the logistical questions.

"Where were you stationed?"

Germany. But I actually ended up spending more time in Iraq.

"Did you actually...you know, kick down doors and stuff?"

Yes. I was in the infantry.

"How long were you in the Army?"

Almost 5 years. I signed up for 4 but was stop lossed.

The logistical questions were easy to answer. Anyone else from the Midwest understands that our conversations are built on small talk, and the best small talk is predicated upon logistical data. How long was the flight? Where did you buy that shirt? For how much? It rained 2 days ago. No, I'm mistaken. It rained 3 days ago. How old is your son? How many kids? I'm not asking if you're hungry, I'm wondering how long ago you last ate. We're eating in 2 hours. Not only is small talk polite, but it makes language into a comfortable and familiar meeting place where facts beget facts and everyone has equal access to the common denominator of experience. It has a socially-leveling effect. I don't want you to lord your opinions of obscure authors or arcane music over me, I just want to know if you prefer a hard or soft pillow. Because the world we inhabit together, the parts that we hold in common, are composed of the mundane. And so if Midwestern Logistical Small Talk seems humble, it also cleverly hides a secret idealistic heart that presumes all of us, everyone, has a world to share. It's a pragmatic type of communion.

I landed in Brooklyn after the war, where Midwestern Logistical Small Talk was mistaken for stupidity. In his essay "What Was the Hipster?", Mark Greif describes the common social denominator that bound together the superficially diverse traits of the last youth movement (if a shift in stylistic emphasis even deserves to be called a movement) as a desultory knowingness rooted in consumerism. In a complicated labyrinth of sophisticated consumer desires, taste is a substitute for wisdom. Taste – with all of its moral weightlessness and novel detachment – can't actually have much significance outside of a six story walk up. It can only exist stranded on islands in Brooklyn and Silver Lake and Austin. Shipwrecked from tradition and denuded of intimacy with the larger culture it feeds off of. However sophisticated it might be or how eloquently it's expressed, it has to exist within a narrow matrix of familiar cultural references. Sun Ra. Alan Partridge. Zizek. The Hairpin. Zadie Smith. Walter Benjamin. Tin Tin. Kraftwerk. The same books in the same neat artistic stacks on the same IKEA shelves. The same music echoing through the same sleek minimalist apartments, quarter-filled with the same mid-century modern furniture. And all this isn't to say that there a mind-numbing conformity doesn't exist among other American people in other American places, but that a tribe which coalesces around the glib spirit of intellectual novelty, desperate for an empty individuation, inevitably becomes spiritually anemic. Worse, they begin to see their spiritual suffering as a strange sort of victory.

You said that irony was the shackles of youth
REM, What's the Frequency Kenneth?

It was a much more dramatic change for me to go from the Army to Brooklyn than it was to go from Missouri to the Army. The total difference can be summed up in the one question I was only asked in Brooklyn and nowhere else. For me, this question became a synecdoche representing the vast space between American cultures.

Why did you join the Army?

It was half meant as an accusation.

Why did you join the Army?

It's not something to do. I remember one particularly confusing conversation where the person I was talking to almost literally couldn't hear what I was saying:

Why did you join the Army if you're an aspiring writer?

It seemed like a better thing to do than going to the University of Iowa.

A long blank stare.

You went to Iowa?

...No...I joined the Army.

It's not something to do. Who does it? The Eastern Seaboard has one of the lowest rates of enlistment in the country. Imagine what the rate must be among graduates of Liberal Arts colleges living in Brooklyn. It's nearly incomprehensible that someone would enlist in the Army.

Why did you join the Army?

I signaled as if I was in their tribe. I watched *Solaris* and even read *Roadside Picnic*. I had a subscription to the New York Review of Books and maybe I would mention Robert Duncan's The H.D. Book during brunch. These points of reference were constellations used to navigate social waters that were actually never too far from familiar shores for the Brooklyn tribe. The variation within them, whether you prefer this writer over that, was all just the narcissism of small differences. The point was that by even having an opinion existing between a stable orthodoxy of cultural bookends, you were expressing a fundamental commonality. You act like one of us, but we don't join the Army. So why did you?

Why did you join the Army?

It makes sense in the tribe to go to grad school. To spend most of the waking hours of the rest of your life in a classroom. To volunteer overseas for a secular NGO. To not work at all and spend your parents' money instead. To retire when you're 25. To write and publish your memoirs when you're 19. To be too busy meditating and skateboarding to work. To be too busy working at a bookstore to meditate or skateboard. To professionally promote parties. To take workshops about how to grow up. To do anything other than serve in the military.

Why did I join the Army? I didn't know how to answer the question. At least not the way they were asking it in Brooklyn. Of course, I'd been asked before. I'd even been asked by other soldiers while I was in the Army, but then the question had been posed with shades of Midwestern Logistical Small Talk. Here was no critical arrow piercing the heart of the action itself. The question didn't come from some fundamental misunderstanding. They weren't asking why anyone would join the Army at all, but what particular set of circumstances led me to join. More than anything else, it was a way to get to know about someone's life before the Army.

Why did you join up?

My father and grandfather and his father before him all served.

My kids needed healthcare.

I wanted money for college.

My uncle wants me to be a police officer like him and he said this is the best way to go about it.

Underneath each of these answers was a basic agreement (usually) about the honor of the venture. No one joins the military just for money or solely out of love of family. It's too profound and uniquely complex a sacrifice for that. And when a young person tells you they enlisted for adventure, what they really mean is that they went on a quest for meaning – our popular vocabulary being too anemic to support the weight of a desire simultaneously so necessary and recondite. We don't have the words to describe our hunger. We struggle to articulate both the depth of our appetite and what might be required to sate it. And there are a lot of reasons why people join up. Some are unutterable. And of those that we can express, many contradict each other. When it comes to something like swearing loyalty to a warring army during a time of combat, motivations can't necessarily be seen through a Manichean lens.

So I tried to think of the question the Brooklynites should have asked if they really wanted to understand something so alien to them. A question that doesn't emit vague antagonism, but one that could possibly draw us closer together and that we could both learn from. Something that would help us understand each other. One day the question posed itself to me.

Do you miss it?

> Tragedy was forsworn, in ritual denial of the ripe knowledge that we are drawing away from one another, that we share only one thing, share the fear of belonging to another, or to others, or to God; love or money, tender equated in advertising and the world, where only money is currency, and under dead trees and brittle ornaments prehensile hands exchange forgeries of what the heart dare not surrender.
> William Gaddis, *The Recognitions*

Sebastian Junger has written a lot about combat. I've overcome my natural revulsion toward the war reporter who longs to go native (unlike everyone else in the situation, they can return to a safe and comfortable home whenever they want – and that's a profound distinction) enough to admit that he gets a lot of things right. The most important thing he gets right is that as horrible as combat is, there are things that soldiers miss about their experiences. Junger writes that:

> ...one of the unacknowledged things that is really complicated for [veterans] is that they get home out of this hell hole and they find that, actually, home is less comfortable than where they'd come from. These guys get back to civilian society and

suddenly the relations they have with those around them, those relations are not solid. They're open to ambiguity and interpretation. And they kind of long for the dangerous security of the bond that happens in a small outpost that's under attack almost every day.

"The dangerous security" is an interesting turn of phrase. And an accurate one. War is something so simple that it becomes profound. The clichés about it are all true, but they're not the whole truth. To say that war is long stretches of boredom punctuated by brief moments of abject terror is generally true. There's a recognizable truth in it. But it's a kind of weightless truth. A stage set that resembles a building but isn't anything anyone could ever actually live in. It's truth in only two dimensions.

War is the most boring thing you can possibly experience. But it makes you into a connoisseur of boredom. You begin to see the intricate patterns of your own mind at work inside of the boredom itself. Nervous staccato rhythms of thought droop into languid melodies. Your reveries eventually feel less desperate. You're no longer lost inside of vast segments of time, but somehow have yourself become part of the flux. You've adapted to it. The boredom is still boredom, only it's become interesting and natural feeling. I spent 16 months in Iraq during my first deployment and I only remember a handful of moments. The rest were spent wandering inside of my own head, becoming more and more intimate with the shape of my fears, desires and dreams. Walter Benjamin called this type of boredom "The dream bird that hatches the egg of experience."

Compared to the shocking fascination of boredom, the violence of war felt banal, even scripted. Maybe it's different for some. The adrenaline high of avoiding and inflicting danger can be an addictive narcotic. But to see a bullet hit someone is to see a person transformed into a body. The thing-ification of a human being and the closing of possibility.

> *...the horses*
> *Rattled the empty chariots through the files of battle,*
> *Longing for their noble drivers. But they on the ground*
> *Lay, dearer to the vultures than to their wives*

That phrase from The Iliad, "dearer to the vultures," has always for me been the bedrock reality of war. Whether or not it's politically necessary or morally defensible has nothing to do with this basic truth: force turns people into objects. And death turns us into the ultimate object. A corpse. A twisted mess of exposed nerves and splintered bone. Simone Weil wrote about this eloquently in The Iliad, or The Poem of Force. She writes about the human spirit being "swept away" or "modified" by the violence of war, "deformed by the weight of it." She writes that, "[t]o define force – it is that x that turns anybody who is subjected to it into a thing...Somebody was here, and the next minute there is nobody here at all..." That part of war, the competition to depopulate the world, doesn't hold much interest for me. It didn't in the moment, and it doesn't now in retrospect. But there's a lot more that happens while living with a small group of people for long stretches of time in a foreign and dangerous place than is spoken of in The Iliad. The experience of war can't be reduced to the experience of force.

My first deployment was 16 months long and my second was 12 months. You dream of home when you're gone for so long, but the home you dream of and how you dream of it become disfigured by time. Remembering and forgetting are bound up together and happen both at once. There was a 24-hour diner that I went to during high school and college where I would escape late suburban nights and order pots of coffee and French fries covered in a plastic neon cheese that would stick to the roof of your mouth. I would sit at a table and read Kerouac for the same reasons that any young person reads Kerouac. I'd discovered him mentioned in the liner notes of a Doors album, and for a long time during high school I was the only person I knew who knew of him. So I was ignorant of the cliche of reading Kerouac at night in a diner while drinking coffee. The experience was fresh to me, and I studied his books like naval captains pour over oceanographic maps. The diner itself wasn't an escape, but felt like a holding pen. Or the airlock of a spaceship. Evidence that somewhere else was possible.

At the beginning of my first deployment I missed the familiarity of the diner. The look of a particular waitress who, wearing her doily-aproned work uniform, appeared much older than she actually was. The cheese on the roof of my mouth. Recognizing the faces of friends through the large glass-walled windows moments before they swung through the double-door entryway. The copper bullet shape of the coffee carafes. Over time, though, the diner had been completely emptied of specificity in my mind, replaced by inchoate desire. By the end of the deployment, I was just sentimental about my dreams of the diner.

Intimacy was responsible for the transformation. Through hours of conversation in small places – in Bradley Fighting Vehicles or guard towers or bunk to bunk – we had articulated these things to each other. Odd confessions, secrets and memories freely wandering inside of our boredom. Not to pass the time necessarily, but to almost alchemically change the medium of time into dense intimate reverie. It was like the weight and importance of our communion in war had retroactively reshaped our memories of home. It had taken simple nostalgia and charged it with more meaning than it could handle. Maybe once or twice in civilian life such conversations were possible. Within the boredom of war, they almost became the norm.

Boys and girls in America have such a sad time together;

sophistication demands that they submit to sex immediately without proper preliminary talk. Not courting talk – real straight talk about souls, for life is holy and every moment is precious.
Kerouac, *On the Road*

The boredom turns out to have been good, and the intimacy that we found inside of it is next to impossible in the world that we would return to. I went back to the diner and it wasn't the same. The coffee was just coffee. The waitress was rude. My friends had stopped coming. Eventually the property was eaten up by the expansion of a car dealership. This was more than a case of "you can't go home again." What Ezra Pound called the "trench-confessions" of war had given the diner meaning. The boredom of war had made these confessions possible. We've been told that a lot of the things we experienced in the war were damaging. A lot of those things might actually be necessary. Or even gifts.

In civilian life you're made to sort through all the war experiences that people tell you are responsible for your dissatisfaction. You're told that it was the war itself which wrecked you and not your return to the commodified world, shallow and brutal as it is. Maybe you'll be cast as a victim, wounded forever. Maybe you'll be a villain. Or crazy. Damaged. A ghost from a world bereft of coherence and value. But you probably know better. The "dangerous security" that Junger mentioned will follow you like a guilty secret pleasure. And you'll long for the truths you learned there together.

As if you could kill time without injuring eternity
Henry David Thoreau, *Walden*

War is mostly boredom. Maybe the quality of the boredom is different in different wars, but for an occupying force like the American Army in Iraq, it was mostly waiting.

Or, really, preparation. Clean your weapon. Service your vehicle. Square your equipment away. Tower guard. Hours and hours of tower guard. The cloudless Iraqi sky nearly as brown as the ground below. Years of your life spent staring into it, endlessly shuffling through your consciousness and dreams and lustful reveries until your thoughts felt alien to you. Like how handling a word too much strips away everything but the sound, tower guard gives you the bizarre resonance of your own mind.

The point of tower guard isn't to dream, obviously. Just the opposite. The point is to cultivate awareness. You scan your field of fire and take in the nuances of your surroundings. The rooftops, sometimes with women hanging laundry. The cars in primary, sun-faded colors. The streets full of humans moving together like a single organism. The contrapuntal darting of children augmenting the primary movement of people in the street below. Or in the countryside. The slow movement of shadows. The distant dust of other American patrols like clouds on the horizon too weak to raise themselves into the sky. The muffled dry hum of faraway noises harmonizing into ambiance.

All together the details form a pattern to familiarize yourself with. You were to know the pattern of things in order to notice deviations. The man standing still on the corner of the building and staring down into the street. The white pickup truck stopped at a crossroads in the distance. The flat, green, night vision rendering of a man slinking into a canal. What preserved your focus through the monotony of tower guard was the knowledge that if you missed something important, your friends would die. Stare too long into the stars and you give someone just enough time to place an IED at the crossroads. Doze off for a few moments and later that day you could be gathering pieces of your friend to send home. In this sense, boredom was really a kind of immersion in the environment. Merleau-Ponty mentions the artist Cezanne's immersion into the landscape, beginning with detailed attention and moving toward a kind of existential crescendo of pure contemplation: "He would start by discovering the geological structure of the landscape; then, according to Mme Cezanne, he would halt and gaze, eyes dilated...'The landscape thinks itself in me,' he said, 'and I am its consciousness.'" What was true for the painter is truer in a broader sense for the soldier peering out of his guard tower, though their intentions are different. Boredom becomes an intervening subject through which we're able to commune with things – objects, memories, notions – beyond our immediate experience. The boredom was dense, but it was also the medium our hopes and fears moved through. The boredom wasn't empty. We filled it with meaning. We were wide awake inside of our boredom.

On no fruits here does my hunger feast / But finds in their learned lack the self-same taste.
Mallarme

Bernard Stiegler became a philosopher while spending 5 years in a French prison for armed robbery. While trapped inside the prison walls he found a sort of pragmatic asceticism. The emptiness around him was full and his boredom was useful. He writes:

As the days passed, I was discovering that there is no interior milieu, but only, remaining here in my cell and under their mnesic shape, in a sense in a hollow, the remains, the defaults, the artifices of which the world consists and through which it finds its consistence. I no longer lived in the world, but rather in the absence of a world, which presented itself here not only as a default, but as that which is always in default, and as a necessary default [un défaut qu'il faut] – rather than as a lack [manque].

To be in tower guard is to spend time in Stiegler's cell and to bear a sacral witness to the irreducible world. The silence is muffled by circumstance. Tower guard is a kind of war in miniature. You gather yourself together inside of a vast tediousness in order to focus your mind on a single and supremely worthy objective: Your duty to the people you live with.

War is boredom charged with moral purpose. It's that purpose which energizes the tedium and distinguishes boredom in war from the boredom of the peaceful world. After the war, the problem isn't having nothing to do, but having nothing that seems worth doing. The boredom of war is simply a banal fact that lays on top of a formidable and captivating reservoir of vital commitments. The boredom of civilian life is the exact opposite. A mesmerizing husk inadequately covering an infinite regression of banality.

Who experienced this regression more acutely than David Foster Wallace? Wallace, the hulking genius who walked away from the unfinished manuscript later published as *The Pale King* in order to take his own life. The partially-finished book that he left us describes how boredom permeates the lives of IRS agents working in a Peoria, Illinois regional examination center. Typically Wallace, the narrative fragments into an undulation of perspectives and plots. It's nearly psychedelic and far too entertaining for a book about boredom. To weigh it down and ground it in boredom – to make the structure cohere to the content a la any postmodern author – there's much space given to the mundane facts of tax assessment. Wallace wants the reader to actually experience boredom firsthand. It's an obviously brave move for an author also trying to sell books. But one guesses that Wallace knew he'd reached a point in his career where reputation preceded and insulated him. He had earned his artistic freedom.

Maybe dullness is associated with psychic pain because something that's dull or opaque fails to provide enough stimulation to distract people from some other, deeper type of pain that is always there...surely something must lie behind not just Muzak in dull or tedious places anymore but now also actual TV in waiting rooms, supermarkets' checkouts, airports' gates, SUVs' backseats. Walkmen, iPods, BlackBerries, cell phones that attach to your head. This terror of silence with nothing diverting to do.

David Foster Wallace, *The Pale King*

The terror of silence with nothing to do. Wallace knew that boredom wasn't just a state, but a fear. The fear of meaninglessness.

Boredom pulls us in two directions at once. On a superficial level it shepherds our attention toward a desire to do something – anything – else. On a deeper level, it distracts us from a profound confrontation with the need to direct our lives toward a core purpose. The characters in *The Pale King* look for meaning in the past, in stories of their own often brutal and traumatic childhoods. They look for meaning in their jobs with the IRS. Wallace writes in the book:

I learned that the world of men as it exists today is a bureaucracy. This is an obvious truth, of course, though it is also one the ignorance of which causes great suffering. But moreover, I discovered, in the only way that a man ever really learns anything important, the real skill that is required to succeed in a bureaucracy. I mean really succeed: do good, make a difference, serve. I discovered the key. This key is not efficiency, or probity, or insight, or wisdom. It is not political cunning, interpersonal skills, raw IQ, loyalty, vision, or any of the qualities that the bureaucratic world calls virtues, and tests for. The key is a certain capacity that underlies all these qualities, rather the way that an ability to breathe and pump blood underlies all thought and action. The underlying bureaucratic key is the ability to deal with boredom. To function effectively in an environment that precludes everything vital and human. To breathe, so to speak, without air. The key is the ability, whether innate or conditioned, to find the other side of the rote, the picayune, the meaningless, the repetitive, the pointlessly complex. To be, in a word, unborable. It is the key to modern life. If you are immune to boredom, there is literally nothing you cannot accomplish.

What he means is that the key to surviving the boredom of modern life is to ignore your appetite for meaning and purpose. You'll be able to do anything. The tradeoff is that it won't matter very much.

Boredom is a distraction from our constant battle against nihilism. Seen this way, it's also sort of an extension of nihilism itself. A spiritual torpor the early Christian Fathers called Acedia. The Latin acedia comes from the Greek akèdia, or "lack of care." Franciscan Bernard Forthomme wrote that the etymological history of the word is based on the neglect of burying one's dead – and so the somewhat diluted horror of our contemporary boredom is predicated upon the savagery of an unburied corpse left bloating in the sun. Maybe you recognize the face, but you've neglected the responsibilities that give form to your humanness and have left the body to be gnawed at by animals and the wind. This abdication of responsibility forms the foundation of boredom. This is the atrocious root of its significance.

The ancient Christian desert fathers considered Acedia, or the noonday demon, an abdication of spiritual responsibilities. Carelessness in a tragically sublime register. Evagrius of Pontus, author of *On The Eight Thoughts*, wrote that Acedia:

...attacks the monk...and besieges his soul...First of all, he makes it appear that the sun moves slowly or not at all, and that the day seems to be fifty hours long. Then he compels the monk to look constantly toward the windows, to jump out of the cell...And further, he instills in him a dislike for the place and for the state of life itself, for manual labor, and also the idea that love has disappeared from the brothers and there is no one to console him...[the demon] leads him on to a desire for other places where he can easily find the wherewithal to meet his needs and pursue a trade that is easier and more productive.

Jean-Charles Nault reminds us in *The Noonday Devil* that Acedia has two dimensions: one temporal, the other spatial. Time distends into a languid desert. Space contracts into a suffocating prison. The spiritual disease initially manifests as restlessness, causing the monk to want to wander around searching for anything to occupy his idle mind. The second manifestation is a focus on the body. This can be a kind of hypochondria or even, shockingly, gluttony. The third is an aversion to manual work. Unable to qualify the tedium within any context which might give it a larger significance, all work becomes rote. The next manifestation is a little more difficult for a modern mind to understand: neglecting monastic duties. Every little responsibility feels like an unbearable demand. And the final manifestation is a sort of general discouragement through which, according to Nault, "Acedia then urges the monk to abandon the holy way of the heroes, the place where he is residing...in other words, abandon the place of spiritual battle."

It isn't fair to say that monks in the desert might experience boredom on a grand scale but we don't. We have the same torpor in our own lives, sullen and at best distracted in our secular world. The only difference is that our embrace of transcendent moral or spiritual goals is no longer explicit, and so we've collectively forgotten that they exist as human needs. We suffer the same maladies, but no longer have the means to reorient and cure ourselves. What Nault lists as the manifestations of Acedia:

restlessness, obsession with the body, dissatisfaction with work and abandonment of the search for deep meaning – are all traits of our contemporary world. We've created a society based on the cultivation of Acedia. We gorge ourselves on triviality and call our insatiability freedom.

The philosopher Byung-Chul Han writes in *The Burnout Society* that:

We owe the cultural achievements of humanity – which include philosophy – to deep contemplative action. Culture presumes an environment in which deep attention is possible. Increasingly, such immersive reflection is being displaced by an entirely different form of attention: hyperattention. A rash change of focus between different tasks, sources of information, and processes characterizes this scattered mode of awareness. Since it also has a low tolerance for boredom, it does not admit the profound idleness that benefits the creative process...If sleep represents the high point of bodily relaxation, deep boredom is the peak of mental relaxation. A purely hectic rush produces nothing new.

Han goes on to say that the cure for boredom with walking isn't running, but dancing. The cure for boredom with triviality isn't a quantifiable increase in frenetic movement, but a deeper meaning in each movement itself.

I spent a lot of time on rooftops in Brooklyn after the war. People would gather there to have parties, cookouts or smoke cigarettes in the sun. Sometimes I would stand at a corner of the roof and imagine I was back on guard tower, scanning my sectors of fire. The horizon was filled with color and undulated with the movement of the city. But I was never able to penetrate beyond the frenetic emptiness of the skyline. Like a thin layer you could peel back to reveal, not a void, but an endless series of thin phenomenological husks. In the desert I had found purpose behind the boredom. In the city I found a frenetic emptiness.

Look me in the eyes and tell me that I'm satisfied.
The Replacements, Unsatisfied

Chapter 2

Ritual

I was an infantryman. Or maybe it's more accurate to say that I am an infantryman still. I'm not sure what the other military operations specialties were like, but being an infantryman is more than a job or a career designation. That was made very clear to me from the beginning, when I came to the Armed Forces Recruiting Center, awkwardly nestled in a suburban St Louis strip mall. I wanted to join the infantry. My reasoning was that there didn't seem to be a point in joining the Army if I were just going to do a civilian job during my enlistment. If I wanted to be a cook I could apply at a restaurant. If I wanted to drive a truck, there were civilian companies that offered free training. If I was going to be in the military, I wanted to do something that I could only do in the military.

On the day that I came in to sign my contract, the recruitment NCO who I'd been working with doing background checks and preliminary physical fitness screenings showed me two contracts. One would have made me a UAV pilot stationed in Hawaii. The other an infantry soldier stationed in Germany. I chose the contract for Germany, signed it and began the process of becoming an infantryman.

Any narrative of joining the military is really two parallel stories, each significant in their own contradictory ways. One is a story of paperwork. Contracts are signed, medical records are accrued, forms are processed and there are double-copy records of equipment being issued. A thick stack of paperwork begins to accumulate before you even begin basic training, and you'll have to keep track of it until you leave the military and, in many cases, even afterwards. The American military is one of the world's largest bureaucracies, employing millions of people and utilizing billions of dollars' worth of equipment which are in turn shadowed by reams of paper work. Scott Thomas Beauchamp existed in this world, a shadow world of files and drawers, as a kind of bureaucratic ghost in an army of Social Security numbers.

The other story of joining the Army is a narrative of ritualistic power. Your hand is raised and an oath is taken. Basic Training itself isn't simply an educational course, but an elaborate initiation ritual in which you're made to memorize creeds and songs, transformed and bonded through collectively surviving a crucible. The paperwork follows along your entire military career, but so do the rituals, each overlaying and complementing the other in complex ways. The bureaucracy and paperwork doesn't just (arguably) allow for the smooth functioning of so many desperate individual parts, but also connects the military like a viscous membrane to the civilian world. Ritual works in the opposite direction, drawing the group back into itself. And that's why, even though bureaucracy and ritual are equally important to the functioning of a military, ritual is something that's considered closer to the secret core of the martial experience.

The words "military" and "ritual" feel almost synonymous. That's partially because most civilian experiences of the military are public displays of drill and ceremony – parades, funerals, flag raisings – but also in part because the military experience is so rich with chthonic energy. There's a wild, martial force that demands to be contained by rigid ceremonial structure, and I think that people sense that. The military requires a profound collective sacrifice of its members, and ritual is necessary for us to reach the deepest parts of ourselves together, necessary to make those kinds of sacrifices. Not just physical sacrifices of life and limb, but of social identity as well. And ritual is necessary for both the death of the old self as well as the formation of a new collective identity.

You sign a contract to join up. You get a medical screening. You even raise your right hand and say an oath. But you don't really become an infantryman until you leave home, symbolically die and are ceremonially reborn as an infantryman. This experience of ceremonial self is sort of the inverse of the bureaucratic identity that follows you around the military in the form of a paper trail.

You leave home. You turn over your cell phone and all your civilian things. For me, my civilian bag was locked in a backroom until I graduated from basic training and Advanced Individual Training (AIT). You don't have a name anymore. You have a number and a platoon assignment. B106. C223. Even your appearance is altered. If you wear glasses, you're issued with standardized military eyewear. Your clothes are a uniform. Your head is shaved. Think of the famous scene at the beginning of Stanley Kubrick's *Full Metal Jacket*, with the sad-sack country music twanging while morose or confused looking young men (all young men, because of time and place) endure the "induction cut." Multi-colored clumps of hair cover the floor, which at least symbolically resembles the floor of a slaughterhouse. Anthony Stevens writes in *Archetype Revisited: An Updated Natural History of the Self*:

Military recruit training still embodies the archetypal stages of separation from family, transition through period of testing, indoctrinating and inculcating skills, followed by a ceremony of incorporation...The new recruit joining his unit for basic training ("boot camp") is subjected to a full-scale rite d'entre. He sacrifices his civilian persona as his mother's son, is assigned a military identity and number, made to don the uniform of the initiate ("rookie," "sprog," or "ant") and treated to the notorious military haircut (a symbolic – or perhaps not so symbolic – mutilation).

I don't remember my induction cut. I was probably too nervous for the memory to adhere. One moment I was on my way from the Atlanta airport to Ft Benning, Georgia. My head was against the window and columns of pines moved in and out of the ambient light of the bus. Then drill instructors were waking us up at 4.30 am by banging pots and pans. In total, basic training and AIT was less than 4 months long, but time distended in immediate experience and memory to make it commensurate with the heft of its significance. It felt as if it went on for years.

I don't remember the exact symbolic moment when I was no longer a civilian. I do remember the night that I became an infantryman.

We had just spent over a week performing our final field exercise, or FTX. Everything we'd learned during basic training and AIT had been implemented in the exercise: battle drills, marksmanship, bivouacking, etc. Late autumn in Western Georgia isn't as warm as you might think, especially if you're sleeping on the ground at night. I piled dead leaves around my sleeping bag to help trap in heat, taking extra care not to crunch around in them. Noise and light discipline was something else we'd learned. One night the roving guard keeping watch around our camp while we slept saw a wild boar and people scampered up trees.

During the day we fought mock battles and raided hastily constructed cheap plywood huts. We responded to simulated medical emergencies. We learned about spotting rudimentary booby traps. There was even a fake tower guard to prepare us for what the drill sergeants, who had almost all deployed to Iraq or Afghanistan themselves, knew would take up a bulk of a lower ranking enlisted infantryman's time overseas. Everything we'd been painfully and meticulously trained to do was implemented. It didn't feel like a final test. It felt more like the drill sergeants showing us who we were now, convincing us of what we were capable of. All the tests were behind us.

The last field exercise ended with a night march that spiraled up a rust colored dirt path on a large hill swaying with new growth pines. In our night vision goggles the trees looked like one-dimensional paper cutouts, the crudely painted backdrop of a children's play or a puppet show. And even though this was the longest march during basic training, and almost entirely up an incline, the general mood was ecstatic. We struggled to maintain the sound discipline that we'd been practicing during our FTX. Everyone was so giddy we could hardly keep our mouths shut. Rumors had been circulating for weeks that this was it. After we marched the "Stairway To Heaven" as it was colloquially known, we'd be inducted into the brotherhood of the infantry by way of a powerful and mysterious ceremony. But if the military moves on its stomach, as Napoleon said, it also moves with an ear to the ground, living off of rumors both hopeful and cynically pessimistic. We didn't know what to expect exactly, just that something was coming.

When we reached the top of the hill, we stood in darkened formation and dropped our gear until we were simply wearing our camo uniforms. A drill sergeant told us to grab our metal canteen cups and fall out of formation to form a single file line. Tiki torches marked a path toward large metal bowls full of something called Infantryman's Grog (most likely just a few sodas and fruit juices mixed together), which we dipped our canteen cups in before precariously shuffling into a large clearing and reorganizing into ad hoc platoon formations. Our drill sergeants stood half in shadows at the edge of the clearing, impassively observing us. Any lingering cynicism I might have been carrying toward the pomp and circumstances of military had momentarily dissipated. I felt empty and new. Freed from irony and suffused with purpose. The vault of the sky felt within reach.

Once we were assembled, the drill sergeants sternly prompted us to sing the Infantryman Song:

You can hear it in the heat of the jungle
You can hear it across the sea
It calls to every freedom loving man
The cry of the US Infantry
Follow Me! Follow Me!
From Concord Bridge to An Khe Ridge
Through the swamps and mountains and sand
They fight and die where brave men lie
Against all tyrants they stand
You can hear it in the heat of the jungle
You can hear it across the sea
It calls to every freedom loving man
The cry of the US Infantry
Follow Me! Follow Me!

Our voices were edgy with excitement. We'd been memorizing and singing the song since the beginning of basic training, but on that night it finally felt like we were actually singing about ourselves, about a group that we belonged to. Our voices fell away and there was a beat of heavy silence before a drill sergeant, face still touched with fire and shadows, prompted us to recite the Infantryman Creed:

I am the Infantry.
I am my country's strength in War,
her deterrent in peace.
I am the heart of the fight –
wherever, whenever.
I carry America's faith and honor
against her enemies.
I am the queen of Battle.
I am what my country expects me to be –
the best trained soldier in the world.
In the race for victory,

I am swift, determined, and courageous,
armed with a fierce will to win.
Never will I fail my country's trust.
Always I fought on –
through the foe,
to the objective,
to triumph over all.
If necessary, I fight to my death.
By my steadfast courage,
I have won 200 years of freedom.
I yield not:
to hunger,
to cowardice,
to fatigue,
to superior odds,
for I am mentally tough, physically strong,
and morally straight.
I forsake not –
my country,
my mission,
my comrades,
my sacred duty.
I am relentless
I am always there,
now and forever.
I AM THE INFANTRY!
FOLLOW ME!

The song and creed were not perfunctory. They took on the power of incantation, simultaneously affirming our new status as infantrymen and conjuring some concrete collective manifestation of our identity.

The drill sergeants spoke to us from the front of our formation. Our first sergeant began, explaining the significance of the ceremony and emphasizing how irrevocably our lives were changed. We were new men, shorn of our civilian identities and reborn into a brotherhood that seemed to stretch back not just to The Battle of The Bulge and Yorktown, but into the distant and half-forgotten roots of civilization itself. We were initiates into a tribe that seemed to stand adjacent to historical time, strengthened by its detachment from what we had left behind in the civilian world. And after our platoon sergeant spoke to us, reiterating the liminal nature of the event and the chasm now separating us from our former lives, he embraced each of us one by one pledging loyalty unto death. It was the most profound and mystical experience of my life.

It's also something that sounds absurd, at best, when explained to civilians. In the worst case it sounds quasi-fascist. Torches, blood, ahistorical renderings of identity. And, of course, the problematic nature of ritual itself. Ritual still exists in contemporary civilian culture, of course, albeit in forms mostly denuded of their metaphysical coherence and inflected with a destabilizing sense of irony. We still throw birthday parties, give out Halloween candy and perform an ever-decreasing number of religious rituals, but the rituals themselves don't seem necessary to the functioning of the world. Quite the opposite, in fact. It feels as if the detached irony of modernity allows us to truly understand the ritual and not the other way around. And so to tell people that, seen from the inside, the ritual "works" in a way that would require an existential shift in their own feeling, thinking and being to comprehend simply confirms their bias against it. What they hear is, "It makes sense if you stop thinking about it." But the narrowness of that critique not only suggests a lack of imagination about how humans embody truth in the world, but ignores the force and energy of my own firsthand experiences – both the power of the ritual and the sad emptiness of a world without it.

Many felt a profound malaise at the idea that the sources of benevolence should be just enlightened self-interest, or simply feelings of sympathy. This seemed to neglect altogether the human power of self-transcendence, the capacity to go beyond self-related desire altogether and follow a higher aspiration.

Charles Taylor, *A Secular Age*

The literature on ritual is vast and complex. Definitions of what ritual is are narrowed or broadened depending on the intentions of the writer. But it's safe to say that the historical record definitively shows that ritualistic behavior, like music and art, is fundamental to being human. And to think about ritual is to reflect on the architecture of human culture itself, how it creates and expresses values and meaning. Which is also to say that ritual is something you do, it's an action, but it's an action that creates or reinforces symbolic meaning. As professor of religious studies Barry Stephenson writes, "Ritual is not only something that people (and animals) engage in; it is also a way of regarding things. Ritual is both action and idea, and this fact can make it a slippery fish."

Stephenson mentions animals, and that's usually what our minds turn to when we think of ritual. The mindless, quasi-instinct aspect of it usually means a devaluation of ritual in the contemporary mind. Something devoid of thought and so also of value. Hence the word "ritual" itself having become something of a synonym for rote, mechanical activity that's almost entirely devoid of meaning. But the power of ritual lies in the subtlety of nonverbal discourse (even if specific language is invoked in the ritual itself), and that's not something that's easily evoked in the kind of self-centered, emotivist language we use to describe our lives. Julian Huxley first introduced the concept of animal ritualization in a now famous 1914 paper Courtship Habits of the Great Crested Grebe. The paper was notable for distinguishing between communicative and instrumental behavior; that is, between ritualized behavior meant to communicate information (such as the dance that bees do to relay where pollen is) and ritualized behavior meant to enact physical change in an animal's environment (nest building, for instance), but also for showing how these two aspects of ritual often blend and reinforce one another. In the case of the Great Crested Grebe, the elaborate dance in which they mirror one another, dancing through the water in an intricate rhythm until finally rising in synchronicity to flit across the surface, a willingness to mate is communicated as the social bond which accompanies the mating is simultaneously deepened.

It isn't so much that our dry observational language perfectly conveys that meaning of the dance, but that in describing the value and beauty of the dance, our everyday language distends and warps into something approaching the poetic. As if ritual itself shakes our language to life, or at least reorients it toward some hidden depth.

Perhaps this happens because ritual is older than language. Older than civilization itself. A major prerequisite of the so-called Great Leap Forward, the dramatic schism humans experienced from their more brutal animalistic past during the Paleolithic era in which all the things we associate with being human were developed – art, music, language – might have been ritual. The writing of people such as Mircea Eliade and J.D. Lewis-Williams suggest that the oldest art we've found, cave paintings, should be interpreted through a spiritual shamanistic lens. In the story they tell, tens of thousands of years ago, humans in slightly hallucinatory reveries descended into caves to convey in fixed form the mysteries they had been inducted into – perhaps by a leader or priestly caste. This knowledge was touched by the transmogrified sacred setting of the cave and the sense that what was occurring was happening in a parallel time. The knowledge a vertical knowledge, not the horizontal lessons of knot tying, hunting or building, but the deeply occult sensation of consciousness becoming aware of itself. As Barry Stephenson writes, "The impulse to leave the daily world of light and safety for the dangers of the cave suggest an urge to seek out a distinct place for extraordinary acts, a place that by virtue of its very separation from ordinary life was perhaps thought to offer knowledge and experience of the world in its totality." So yes, birthday parties and Halloweens are rituals of a sort, but my induction into the brotherhood of the infantry had more in common with our early experiences in the cave. The act of the ritual was evidence of the esoteric complexity of existence itself.

> The strongest hint of something spiritual, some religious ceremony in the cave, is this bear skull. It has been placed dead center on a rock resembling an altar. The staging seems deliberate. The skull faces the entrance of the cave, and around it fragments of charcoal were found, potentially used as incense. What exactly took place here only the painting could tell us.
> Werner Herzog, *Cave of Forgotten Dreams*

Considering the metaphysical weight of cave drawings and induction into the infantry, it seems useful to differentiate those things from contemporary ceremony – birthday parties, Halloween, etc. The distinction is stark for anyone who has lived the difference, but for those who haven't, the line separating ritual and ceremony might be difficult to make out. In my own experience, the difference between the two lies in the difference between invocation and confirmation of the pre-existing. Ritual invokes or creates as it simultaneously confirms. Ceremony is a formalized process of confirmation. By this definition, ritual seems closer to magic or religion.

The anthropologist Michael Houseman writes that "ritual action is, if it is fficacious...irreversibly effects ordinary intercourse in perceptible ways: before and after are not the same. From this point of view, ritualization is serious business, its efficacy quite different from the gratification that results from playing (or observing) a game or from observing (or participating in) a spectacle." Houseman's distinction suggests that ritual, unlike ceremony, fundamentally changes reality. Ceremony seems simply a more complete confirmation of a fuller reality.

Anthropologist Victor Turner famously defined ritual as "formal behavior prescribed for occasions not given over to technological routine that have reference to beliefs in mystical beings or powers." Definitions, of course, simultaneously hide while they conceal. And while Turner's definition might be narrower than others, it does emphasize, with its "beliefs" and "powers," the religious element that I myself found so inseparable from ritual. The military isn't a religion, but it's obvious to anyone with even a passing familiarity that there is a quasi-mystical sense about things that grow in power the closer one gets to the battlefield, death and an awareness of profound sacrifice. As Turner suggests, ritual requires belief. In my case, that belief wasn't necessarily in ourselves or the skills we learned as infantry recruits, but rather it was a belief that moved through us, that guided us toward something like a transcendence of self. We hadn't just died to our former civilian lives during basic training. We had also died to the notion that individuality trumps all. And as for not being given over to "technological routine," you can't get more outside the purview of either of those terms than approaching patriarchal leadership by fire light. Even if basic training itself meant learning how to use radios and shoot weapons, we weren't allowed to call ourselves infantrymen until we ascended a hill at night, a pilgrimage to a center of power where we would lose ourselves in order to gain admittance to another world.

You know sometimes I say to myself, if every single day, at

exactly the same stroke of the clock one were to perform the same act, like a ritual, unchanging, systematic, every day at the same time, the world would be changed.
Andrei Tarkovsky, *The Sacrifice*

Ritual is a way of understanding. A way of knowing that bypasses the rational mind. It's a knowing with the body, with action, with location and with a will to believe. The post-Enlightenment emphasis on a Cartesian split between mind and body devalued the power of ritual in popular consciousness simply by extracting our actions from the ontological ground of being which would imbue them with transcendent meaning. Michel Foucault differentiated philosophy from spirituality by writing that in spirituality, "the subject carries out the necessary transformations on himself in order to have access to truth." Philosophy, meanwhile, "is the form of thought that asks what it is that enables the subject to have access to the truth and which attempts to determine the conditions and limits to the subject's access to the truth." Of course, Foucault also points out that in ancient forms of thought, this bifurcation didn't exist. As Barry Stephenson writes, "The question of how to have access to the truth and ritual as a transformative practice allowing access to the truth were not separated."

In other words, the unique value of the "authentic" work of art has its basis in ritual, the location of its original use value. This ritualistic basis, however remote, is still recognizable as secularized ritual even in the most profane forms of the cult of beauty.
Walter Benjamin, *The Work of Art in the Age of Mechanical Reproduction*

My mind returns to the reams of paperwork that follow you around your entire military career, past it even and into civilian life as a bureaucratic record of your time in the service. If the initial contract you sign is where all of that begins, where does its counterpoint start? Where does the ritual begin? I suppose it starts with the oath that every prospective service member raises their right hand and swears before shipping off to basic. For me, it was the first oath I'd ever taken, and it was startling in its primal simplicity:

> I, Scott Beauchamp, do solemnly swear that I will support and defend the Constitution of the United States against all enemies, foreign and domestic; that I will bear true faith and allegiance to the same; and that I will obey the orders of the President of the United States and the orders of the officers appointed over me, according to regulations and the Uniform Code of Military Justice. So help me God.

Signing the contract felt like a formality, but swearing the oath felt like a true introduction. Maybe that's because the contract felt like an artifact from the civilian world, a banal necessity that had more to do with civilian oversight than the martial experience itself. Which isn't entirely true, of course. It'd be impossible to properly feed, clothe and equip the troops without it. But the purpose of the oath cut deeper than efficient instrumentality. Embedded in it is the existential grounding that gives purpose to military sacrifice in the first place.

The oath felt important to me, but what is it exactly? How does it function in relation to the contract I had signed? Giorgio Agamben, in his enigmatic text *The Sacrament of Language: An Archeology of the Oath*, defines the oath as "...a linguistic act intended to confirm a meaningful proposition (a dictum), whose truth or effectiveness it guarantees." Agamben emphasizes the point that oaths themselves don't "produce a new and particular obligation," but instead provide a sort of verbal covenant. Language willing its own adherence to truth. A kind of linguistic ritual writ small.

What the oath reminded me of was an incantation signifying fealty to the very idea of moral truth. The oath was an invocation of ontological coherence itself. In writing about the ancient sources of the oath, Agamben mentions it as among the first-principles of the pre-Socratic philosophers, "as if the origins of the cosmos and of the thought that understands it implied the oath in some way." The oath is categorized as something ancient, something that the gods themselves are subject to. And so, Agamben reasons, the oath (like the ritual), suggests something radical by its very existence. He writes that:

> ...perhaps our entire habitual way of representing to ourselves the chronological and conceptual relationship between law and religion must be revised. Perhaps the oath presents to us a phenomenon that is not, in itself, either (solely) juridical or (solely) religious but that, precisely for this reason, can permit us to rethink from the beginning what law is and what religion is.

There's a Kids in the Hall sketch that takes place in a courtroom. A frowning lawyer played by Bruce McCulloch determinedly marches to the witness stand where the smiling defendant, Dave Foley, sits with a cup of coffee.

"All right, I'm going to cut right to the legal chase. Did you kill Henry Tillson?" asks McCulloch.

"No. [smiling] This is so easy!" Foley's character laughs before taking another sip from his mug.

The judge suggests that Foley's character retain a lawyer instead of defending himself, but he insists that he's "doing fine."

"Go ahead, ask me another one," he playfully demands.

"Did you kill Henry Tillson?" McCulloch asks again.

"No," Foley grins and impertinently takes another sip.

"Your honor, I'd like to present Exhibit A. Is this your gun?"

"No."

"Yes it is!"

"No it isn't"

"We have your name on the registration."

"No you don't."

"May I remind you that you're under oath!"

"Oh right, and I would never lie under oath. Not to God," Foley beams.

It's a sketch that I've always found as equally disturbing as humorous. What upsets me is the total and utter disregard of the oath – what Agamben portrays as the linguistic act that conjures meaning and order into existence. The mutual foundation of both law and the religious sentiment. Ritual, the scaffolding which constructs the coherence of our shared reality, torn down in a gleeful act of selfish nihilism. In Foley's self-satisfied grin I see the deranged spirit of our contemporary world and its maniacal disavowal of ritual.

> Ritual is not compatible with the rapid rhythm that industrialism has injected into life. So whenever ritual happens in a place commanded by or dominated by a machine, ritual becomes a statement against the very rhythm that feeds the needs of that machine. It makes no difference whether it is a political machine or otherwise.
>
> Malidoma Patrice Somé, *Ritual: Power, Healing and Community*

The military is shot through with ritual. It isn't an exaggeration to say that the ritualistic order is experienced every day, from morning formations to the final trumpet call of "Retreat" that plays on loudspeakers across military installations every evening. And I'd be lying if I said that it wasn't a difficult adjustment for me coming from the civilian world. We think of ritual as empty signification at best, and manipulative at worst. To suggest that we "think" about it too much, instead of wrapping ourselves up in it and experiencing it from the inside, would be to most people's minds a kind of abdication of duty. As if all forms of truth begin and end in conscious thought.

During my first deployment I became enamored with Ezra Pound. I worked my way from Hugh Kenner's *The Pound Era* through the Cantos themselves (with the help of a handy guide) and onto his slender volume on Confucius, with the inadvertent result that I came to feel more at ease with ritual. In *The Book of Rites*, Confucius describes an ancient period of disharmony, an anarchic hell full of egotism and rampant crime. The world was restored to order through a series of Li, often translated as "ceremony." Li brought form back to the world by binding people together through the ritualistic act. Barry Stephenson writes that:

> Anticipating Durkheim by more than two millennia, the Liji [or Book of Rites] claims that ritual has the capacity to organize otherwise atomized individuals into a cohesive group. Ritual gets everyone on the team pulling in the same direction, as it were, but it is no guarantee of harmony...Yet ritual is all we have, hence the profound concern in the Liji to both argue the merits of ritual and to understand and explain the conditions under which ritual fails to function as a substitute for "The Great Way" [a sort of prelapsarian time or way of being antecedent to the discord that the Liji is meant to address].

The language of the Liji is almost incomprehensible in our contemporary society, and we usually take the causes of that incomprehensibility as a victory. The world is demystified and something like objective truth is illuminated. And through our pristine mental clarity we're given the ability to stand alone. To cultivate our ego. Moving from the military back to the civilian world was a movement away from interaction with Deep Time to being ensnared in Me Time. Sounds cheesy, and it is. We might have abdicated a shared culture that understands the significance of ritual in order to achieve some kind of sense of freedom, but that shallow, facile freedom is meaningless without a shared ground of being that ritual makes possible. Our ideology of ego is cheesy and cliche, not the rituals we've left behind.

> Each person, withdrawn into himself, behaves as though he is a stranger to the destiny of all the others. His children and his good friends constitute for him the whole of the human species. As for his transactions with fellow citizens, he may mix among them, but he does not feel them; he exists only in himself and for himself alone. And if on these terms there remains in his mind a sense of family, there no longer remains a sense of society.
>
> Alexis de Tocqueville, *Democracy in America*

Of all the aspects of ritual, of all the elements through which its power manifests (liminality, supra-intellectual apprehension of reality, coordinated art expressions, etc.) it's the sense of connection to the group that's most powerful. Mary Douglas writes in Away From Ritual, the first essay of her book *Natural Symbols*, that "One of the gravest problems of our day is the lack of commitment to collective symbols." She goes on to talk about the loss of ritual as just that, a loss, and laments its relatively recent association with "empty conformity." And from what I've seen she's right. But I wonder if ritual being so connected to group bonding might suggest a more problematic chicken and egg question: Did a turn away from ritual predicate the anomie of society, or did the anomie predicate the devaluing of ritual? Of course, ritual won't mean anything to isolated individuals more accurately defined by their consumption habits than by their commitments to each other. Ritual requires community.

Calmer, fitter, healthier, and more productive / A pig in a cage on antibiotics

Radiohead, Fitter Happier

Chapter 3

Community

What was the most scathing insult that a drill sergeant could deliver during basic training?

"You think you're an individual?"

Why did it cut so deeply? Say you decided to roll your socks instead of fold them. Or you casually walked to your destination instead of marching in a formation like you were instructed. Why wouldn't the intimidating figures in their Smokey The Bear hats just yell at you for not following orders or failing to adhere to directions? Why allege a desire to be unique – something that, on its face, doesn't seem like all that of a bad thing. It might even be a simple and obvious fact, like being a human or alive.

How could it be an insult? Why did it penetrate your conscious and make you feel like you were failing not just yourself but your fellow recruits as well? The insult wasn't something you could easily put aside. It was brittle with disdain and heavy with some nebulous disgust at the civilian world you had come from. It seemed a close cousin to its related insult: "You think you're back on the block?" There's something revealing in the resonance between the two insults. One of the most obvious indicators that we were no longer in the civilian world was that now our identities were determined primarily by group. Our martial associations were the new foundation of who we were, and individual traits (personality, experiences, etc.) would be largely subsumed and secondary to that. It wasn't anything like I had experienced in the civilian world. How could it be? It was nearly the opposite.

Even the closest analogies from my own pre-Army life would have been misleading guides to the communal military existence. Football and wrestling teams? Bands? Coworkers?

None of it even began to approach the intensity of collective purpose, intimacy and strength of communal bonds that are necessitated by the military experience. With all of those other things you were always primarily an individual. Even if there was collaboration, that was always secondary to your identity as a lone nodule meandering through the universe. Your isolation was the foundation of your identity. And a sort of freedom, if not the very definition of freedom.

Through my teens and most of my twenties I was romantically adrift in the world. I'd always attributed the rootlessness to youth. Young people are restless, hunting out truer and higher selves through the anemic hunger of contemporary culture, hardly ever finding themselves sated. And so we fall in love with the hunger itself. It felt like an adventure to elevate the significance of each passing experience to as close to mysticism as you can come in our secular world. To allow each starry sky, cup of coffee, road trip or kiss to reverberate in the highest existential register. To let the world move through your own singular vision and let it become itself in detente with your imagination. "The unspeakable visions of the individual," as Kerouac wrote. I understood, though, through each highly stylized moment, that it all felt terribly imbalanced. And it couldn't last. I wouldn't have been able to articulate it at the time, but in retrospect it seems obvious that there was an occult understanding that through my hunger for meaning and belief in "the holy contour of life" (another Kerouac aphorism) I was plunging myself deeper into a sort of spiritual isolation. The shadow side of every romantic youth movement of the past few hundred years was that the more vehemently you went about turning your life into an individual artistic expression, the more you sacrificed in community. The further you cut yourself off from a shared reality. You trade freedom for meaning. For me, life in the military also entailed the long and often painful process of rejoining myself to others.

Not the free individual but the lost individual; not Independence but isolation; not self-discovery but self-obsession; not the conquer but to be conquered; these are major states of mind in contemporary imaginative literature. Robert Nisbet, *The Quest For Community*

I thought I had belonged to communities before I joined the Army, but I hadn't. At least, not in the sense of mid-twentieth century sociologist Robert Nisbet's definition. As he writes in his most famous work, *The Quest For Community*:

In a highly popular statement, we are told that the family has progressed from institution to companionship. But, as Ortega y Gasset has written, "people do not live together merely to be together. They live together to do something together." To suppose that the present family, or any other group, can perpetually vitalize itself through some indwelling affectional tie, in the absence of concrete, perceived functions, is like supposing that the comradely ties of mutual aid which grow up incidentally in a military unit will along outlast a condition in which war is plainly and irrevocably banished. Applied to the family, the argument suggests that affection and personality cultivation can somehow exist in a social vacuum, unsupported by the determining goals and ideals of economic and political society.

A community is how you are useful to each other, how you help each other to survive. Who you are develops from that. It doesn't work in the reverse. According to Nisbet, it can't. Because a group of people who declare themselves a community without being essential to each other aren't a community at all. A social club, perhaps, but they're essential atomized components. Communities are, above all, people who are necessary to each other. And so when we talk about a loss of community, we're talking about becoming obsolete to one other.

Community is a sign that love is possible in a materialistic world where people so often either ignore or fight each other. It is a sign that we don't need a lot of money to be happy – in fact, the opposite.
Jean Vanier, *Community and Growth*

The military isn't the perfect community. Such a thing doesn't exist. The larger purposes that people in the military serve are usually not their own, and in ideal circumstances, the military as an institution doesn't exist for itself. The ends to which the military is put can often be ethically dubious or misguided. But – and this is especially true in the infantry – when you look at the face of another in your platoon, you're inundated by the bone-deep truth that you're there to serve each other. To sustain each other and keep one another alive. Your primary mission might be to close in on and destroy the enemy, but "the enemy" is defined in relation to the harm he might cause the soldiers serving beside you. No army can survive without first being a community.

When my memory falls back unprompted to the time when I served, so much of it is of the gaps between the action and big missions. The bulk of my time in the military was spent eating with people. Sleeping beside them. The sounds I remember are less the recoil of rifles or the barking of orders, and more just laughter and snoring. The sound of humans being together intimately close in space. It isn't abstract or intellectual. And it isn't always enjoyable.

Sleeping in a tent with 20 other men is gross. Especially at night. Especially after having been on a field exercise for weeks or during a long deployment. The smell alone, the oppressive loaminess of feet and dirt veined with the acrid pungency of sweat, is enough to keep you from falling asleep. An off-tempo chorus of snores, some antagonistically tooth-rattling, compete with contra punto bursts of flatulence. Figures stumble around in the darkness searching for the latrine. Guards come in to wake their relief. The muted music of someone who fell asleep with headphones on gently but insistently tugs at your consciousness.

And that's a fairly large tent. Now imagine living for days at a time as part of a three-person crew in a Bradley Fighting Vehicle with its compressed aluminum shell trapping in and amplifying the heat. The plastic bottles full of urine your crew has filled while manning an observation point slowly cook in the ambient heat. Every bodily smell is unique to each person, a heady matrix of the shared rations filtered through each soldier's idiosyncratic body chemistry. Every belch is a fingerprint. Every fart is a snowflake.

But it isn't only the grotesque bodily intimacies that prevail. There's a pervasive simple physical intimacy that I hadn't experienced before or since, not even on sports teams. The easy friendly punch. An arm around the shoulder. Impromptu wrestling. Hair mussing. Yelling across a table. Grabbing things out of each other's hands. Sharing food. Playfully intimidating, this is a rare kind of intimacy in our culture. It's not something I've experienced even with my closest friends, where our emotional intimacy, as deep as it might be, is also heady and abstract. Perhaps I prefer it that way.

There are two easy ways to mis-categorize the profound simplicity of physical intimacy in the military. One is to sexualize it and the other is to abstract it. Both are symptoms of our over-individualized epoch. Intellectuals and others who define themselves through the manipulation of abstract symbols – taken with the notion that since cognition is used to engage with reality, the whole of reality itself must be composed of cognition – always have a difficult time accepting the weighty simplicity of the obvious. Everything disintegrates into esoterica. Or as Etienne Gilson writes about the nature of art as essentially "making" rather than "knowing" in *The Arts of the Beautiful*:

> Idealism is endemic in the minds of philosophers for the simple reason that if reality is our knowledge of it, then we have no need to learn what it is, for it would be enough for the mind to know itself in order to know reality. From the point of view of idealism, since knowledge is all, you cannot pretend that something is not cognition without, by that very fact, sinning against the mind.

Gilson calls this the "sophism of misplaced knowledge." And to call the closeness of men living and fighting together "erotic" is to fall into its trap, revealing more about the final intentions of the interpreter than the experiences of the men themselves.

And then there's the instinct to call the intimacy of war a kind of love similar to Philia, the love shared between friends. But this isn't quite right either. Friends find each other through a shared affinity. People who serve in the military are bonded together by chance. Their fates are entwined by the exigencies of fate. This isn't a "perfect," ideal Platonic love, but something much more chthonic – form below the forms. C.S. Lewis writes in *The Four Loves*, "Need-love cries to God from our poverty; Gift-love longs to serve, or even to suffer for..." If there is love in the messy intimacy of military life, and I think there is because I've felt it, then this is what it is: need-love. It's the affection that you instinctively feel for people whose every day intimacy is a reminder of how necessary you are to each other's existence. This is why the drill sergeant screamed at you in basic training not to act like an individual. Because in the military, in times of combat especially, you survive collectively or not at all. Physical intimacy is just a natural outgrowth of that truth. As well as a constant reminder of it.

War is hell, but that's not the half of it, because war is also mystery and terror and adventure and courage and discovery and holiness and pity and despair and longing and love. War is nasty; war is fun. War is thrilling; war is drudgery. War makes you a man; war makes you dead.

Tim O'Brien, *The Things They Carried*

One of the greatest misconceptions about the Army is that it's one giant amorphous blob. The Big Green Machine. The Borg. All parts connected to each other and communicating perfectly with one another. But anyone who has served a day in their life knows that this isn't the case. The illusion that the entire military is always on the same page is just that. It might look like a single undifferentiated mass from the outside, but it's not. It can't be. And in a counterintuitive twist, it's the variety that exists internally within the military that keeps the anomie of the civilian world at bay.

The military consists of a million and a half people spread over 150 countries around the Earth. The annual defense budget of the Pentagon is something approaching $600 billion, but we can't actually be sure. Even though the law mandates it, they've never been audited. The military itself isn't even quite sure how much property it owns or where it might be located. The image of a multi-tentacled giant cephalopod comes to mind, but that isn't quite right. The American military is more like a spore or fungus, following a genetic imperative to seek out environments where it can meet the basic minimum qualifications for life and to spread. Generals and higher brass might object, insisting that they're in charge, consciously gripping the steering-wheel with white knuckled intensity, lowering their shoulders and forcing this behemoth to go where they want. They flatter themselves. There's a blind, chthonic logic that they're prisoners too as well. They might call it necessity. The politicians that enable them might call it patriotism. A scientist might call it metastasization.

The point is that the military is too large and complex an

organism to be so seamlessly controlled from the top down. There are worlds within worlds within worlds. In her book *How Everything Became War and the Military Became Everything*, law professor and columnist Rosa Brooks describes Fort Carson in Washington state as a kind of universe unto itself:

> The post had everything: a military exchange (the PX) that might have been mistaken for a Walmart, a commissary that stocked multiple varieties of spicy Korean ramen noodles and English crumpets as well as the usual American brands, a Starbucks, a bowling alley, a theater, several gyms and pools, day care centers, a gas station, a post office, a liquor store, three elementary schools and a middle school. Also, of course, there were offices, shooting ranges, barracks for single soldiers, "simulation centers" where soldiers took part in elaborate computerized war games, vast parking lots full of Humvees and tanks, and hangars for helicopters and drones.
>
> Outside Fort Carson's heavily guarded gates was America, in which everything looked exactly the same, except messier. "America" also lacked Fort Carson's occasional grim reminders of the toll taken by a decade of bloody, inconclusive ground wars: tucked neatly between offices, parking lots and children's playgrounds, Fort Carson – which lost more soldiers in Iraq and Afghanistan than any other Army post in the country – also had a "Fallen Heroes Family Center" and a "Wounded Warrior Transition Barracks."

Maybe guys who made a career out of it had a different experience, but for me, my entire time in the military was spent inside of one of these bubbles, stocked as they were to provide for you from birth (hospitals) to death (Fallen Heroes Family Center). We moved a few times, and our unit changed once, but I was with the same guys. We all moved together. The President might have been the Commander in Chief, and there might have been a long and illustrious chain of command leading out of Iraq and Germany and into the inner sanctums of the Pentagon, but they were far beyond the scope of my daily experience. Orders came down from on high, filtered through echelons of middle managers with their own agendas all the way down to our squad and team leaders. The people who knew us and lived with us. There was a certain sort of freedom in this distance – a kind of group or institutional freedom to interpret orders through the lens of our collective experience on the ground. People tried their best to follow orders out of a sense of institutional fealty. But the more distant or abstract the source, the less pressing they seemed. Our deepest sense of loyalty was to each other, starting with the guys to your right and left, the guys in your own squad and platoon, and then dissipating as it radiated outward.

We enter a spiritual puberty where we snap to the fact that the great transcendent horror is loneliness, excluded encagement in the self. Once we've hit this age, we will now give or take anything, wear any mask, to fit, be part-of, not be Alone, we young. The US arts are our guide to inclusion. A how-to. We are shown how to fashion masks of ennui and jaded irony at a young age where the face is fictile enough to assume the shape of whatever it wears. And then it's stuck there, the weary cynicism that saves us from gooey sentiment and unsophisticated naïveté. Sentiment equals naïveté on this continent.

You burn with hunger for food that does not exist.

A US of modern A where the State is not a team or a code, but a sort of sloppy intersection of desires and fears, where the only public consensus a boy must surrender to is the acknowledged primacy of straight-line pursuing this flat and short-sighted idea of personal happiness.

David Foster Wallace, *Infinite Jest*

But Wallace is only half right here. The "US of modern A" might feel barren and lonely, with each of us locked up inside the prison of our individual appetites, free only to gorge ourselves on things that can't possibly sate us. But there is a food for the hunger we were born with, the yearning for deep and unironic connection. It does exist. And I know that it does because I've experienced it and it nourished me. My time in the military was a brief respite from the frivolity of individual caprice.

After typing that, I'm tempted to walk it back, to make a gesture toward acknowledging the power and value of the freedom to pursue our individual desires, atomized and separated from the larger world. I'm tempted to add something like, "Of course, there's a great moral power in being able to feed our individual appetites." Or that being able to choose between two things is the foundation of freedom. But it's a knee-jerk reaction. An empty gesture toward modern convention. And I'm not convinced that it's even necessarily true.

In *No Exit*, Sartre depicts hell as an eternity spent in a drawing room with other people. Consciousness being forced to accommodate itself with the minds of others is as close as Sartre can come to depicting the torments that lie opposite complete freedom. The Look – the awareness of being objectified in the mind's eye of the other – impinges on Sartre's early radically individualized ideation of freedom. That freedom, as Sartre saw it early on in his thinking and writing, was only truly allowed to manifest if it were completely shorn of social and political fetters. Freedom is something that is inert within us by virtue of our individual consciousness. Our social relations, more often than not, distort that freedom. Mute it. Diminish it.

Sartre's freedom is a very modern one. Or at least it feels very contemporary. But it goes back at least to William of Ockham in the twelfth century, who defined freedom as the ability to simply make a choice:

The will is freely able to will something and not to will it. By this I mean that it is able to destroy the willing that it has and produce anew a contrary effect, or it is equally able in itself to continue that same effect and not produce a new one. It is able to do all of this without any prior change in the intellect, or in the will, or in something outside them. The idea is that the will is equal for producing and not producing because, with no difference in antecedent conditions, it is able to produce and not to produce. It is poised equally over contrary effects in such a way in fact, that it is able to cause love or hatred of something...

That might not seem like a very shocking definition of freedom. To modern ears, it might sound like the only viable one. Jean-Charles Nault writes in *The Noonday Devil: Acedia, The Unnamed Evil of our Times*, "It is necessary to realize that Ockham's [conception of freedom] is so ingrained in us today that it is difficult for us to picture freedom as anything other than the possibility to choose between two contradictory things." We're never more free than before we've made a choice, than when we're hanging suspended in the undifferentiated emptiness of our decision, and anything or anyone who limits that choice is impinging on our freedom. The options themselves don't matter much to this definition. In fact, even if something is good, so long as it limits our ability to choose, it limits our freedom.

But there's another, older, definition of freedom which brings us back to the idea of community and of how we should live. That would be something closer to Thomas Aquinas' vision of freedom. Without delving too deeply into the notoriously knotty logic of Scholastic thought, particularly Thomastic Realism, we can simply define this older notion of freedom as our will being directed at what's best for us. Our appetites impressed into the service of cultivating something good. The trick here is that you have to already have defined what "good" is. Aquinas had that. We don't. We've replaced our definitions of the good with process. The choice itself is good. The freedom of the choice is the highest freedom, uninfluenced by habit, convention or monotony. The ends of that freedom overshadowed almost completely by the act itself.

Without a vision of the good, a sort of final end to direct and consecrate our actions, our freedom itself becomes the lonely bars of Wallace's "encagement." We're forever trapped in that strange and empty moment of choosing, unwilling to direct our will to any larger purpose for fear that even that dedication will be enough to sully our naturally unfettered state. To mute our individual freedom.

In our colloquial idea of what it means to be totally free, bending our will toward a transcendent goal – Thomas' God or some grand political ideal – becomes a negation of freedom itself. Or in Sartre's extreme case, even just the penetrating gaze of The Other is enough to puncture our diaphanous sense of complete liberation. The price we pay for this modern idea of freedom then is simultaneously both a sense of meaning and a cultivation of community. We're left atomized and denuded of purpose. And we applaud ourselves.

> *You can do what you want to whenever you want to / You can do what you want to there's no one to stop you...Do what you want to whenever you want to / Though it doesn't mean a thing / Big Nothing*
> Elliot Smith, Ballad of Big Nothing

There's an entire complicated cultural history of why we turned away from the older conception of freedom, away from communal ideas of the common good. This turning away is the entire history of post-Enlightenment politics in the West. It's the entire history of modernity. Freedom is personal freedom or it's nothing.

But there's a shadow trailing this very broad, very simple notion of liberty. It's a wonderful ideal, but, taken to its imaginative limits, can it really exist? What sort of world would we have to live in for every person, in ever scenario, to exist for all time in a freedom completely unrestrained by moral, physical or conceptual fetters? Even taken hypothetically the notion is absurd. We can't have our cake and eat it too. I can't simultaneously move left and right. The Earth has finite resources. The Second Law of Thermodynamics harshly directs the movement of time. Reality imposes limits on our desires as does our own nature – as idiosyncratic and unique as our individual defining characteristics might be. We limit ourselves simply by being one self and not another.

And then there are the very real material limitations imposed on our choices by the culture that we belong to, and an economy predicated in large part upon cultivation of appetite. Our freedom has become in many ways synonymous with consumption. We are the sex we have. We are the music we listen to. The television we watch. The products we buy. Our imaginations, lulled into a fuzzy complacency by the illusion of horizon-less vistas of options, are ensnared in the claustrophobic dream worlds created by universities, marketing agencies and technology firms. The limits within which we dare to imagine our freedom are already dictated, albeit with a gentle touch, by people and institutions with their own largely unexamined motives.

This soft and insidious coercion, all the better hidden for having wrapped itself under the mantle of complete and total human freedom, is Circe-an in its hypnagogic power. The Greek sorceress, daughter of Helios and the sea nymph Perse, is most well-known in our own time for transforming Odysseus' drunk and fattened crew into a herd of pigs. It would be impossible to approach, much less exhaust, the rich depth and variety of meaning alive inside of Book X of The Odyssey – the fundamental unity of all matter, the ancient rules of hospitality, the injunction to trust and respect your captain, the dangers of gluttony – but this rowdy and dissatisfied crew being transformed by intoxicating potions into animals synonymous with self-centered greed is metaphor enough for the freedom we've accepted. The freedom, as Gilles Châtelet wrote, "to think and live like pigs."

> The eighteenth and nineteenth centuries abandoned the idea of spiritual or intellectual happiness in order to have this material happiness, consisting of a certain number of essential consumer goods. And hence, in the nineteenth century, happiness was linked to a well-being obtained by mechanical means, industrial means, production. The new thing that Saint-Just spoke about was that, in the past, happiness could appear as a very vague, very distant prospect for humanity, whereas now, people seemed to be within reach of the concrete, material possibility of attaining it. That was why happiness was to become an absolutely essential image for the nineteenth-century bourgeoisie, and for modern society. Happiness was attainable thanks to industrial development, and this image of happiness brought us fully into the consumer society.
>
> Jacques Ellul, *Perspectives on Our Age*

Without being in service to something larger than itself, our freedom is intoxicating and atomizing. A gluttonous, mind-numbing choice between consumer products which are themselves imbued with an almost metaphysical aura of power. Cheap amulets that promise us self-transcendence without any of the hard work, sacrifice or cost that come with authentic transformation. Factory-made baubles to sate our most profound longings. The co-modification of the best of human culture.

> He beheld Lourdes, contaminated by Mammon, turned into a spot of abomination and perdition, transformed into a huge

bazaar, where everything was sold, masses and souls alike!
Émile Zola, *Lourdes*

The point has been made in poems, rants and songs, at least since Jesus overturned the money changers tables outside of the Temple. And the subtle distinction that I'm making here isn't original, but it's important and bears repeating: There is a kind of freedom in consumer choice and in the open market more broadly. But without something larger than purchasing options, without Ockham's empty moment of decision being constrained by a contest of purpose and values, then freedom becomes empty of significance. Or, worse, a kind of poison which tricks us into thinking that we can buy happiness. That we can purchase meaning. And the burden of that illusion deforms us.

The feeling of walking through the men's clothing section of a large PX on any military base is deadening. Or at least it was for me when I was in active service. Outside of the huge, military-run store, there are flags and monuments hemmed in by fence and gates. Everything outside of the PX speaks to a larger purpose and shared communal sacrifice. Columns of soldiers march by. Retreat is played on speakers across the base at night. The songs of troops running in synchronized groups echoes in unison. But inside of the PX, the men's t-shirts are cheap and gaudy. They're not any different from what you might find in any large box store, but seen in contrast to the solemn purpose of the activities and architecture outside, they're more than depressing. Boastful gold lame words on pre-faded black fabric. Knock-off ironic slogans aping an already long-dead hipster culture. References to TV shows and comics. Lurid manifestations of a pop culture which degrades with flattery.

The desperate gambit at individualism that it offers fails and fails miserably. Real individualism requires an intimacy that isn't for sale. Even in matching uniforms, I could spot the men in my squad and platoon from a distance by their gait. By the outline of their bodies. The way they moved and ran across a field or by the way they drove their Humvee. It's the true and deep knowledge of someone that isn't for sale but can only be purchased with time, pressure, intimacy and knowledge.

I remember a weekend spent in Prague with a few guys from my platoon. In their civilian clothes, some purchased from the PX, they actually seemed to lose the individuality that they had when they were in uniform. What was actually unique about them either blended into the crowd of civilians or was smothered by empty brand consciousness. They disappeared with a miasma of consumer options, and the promise that those options made, that a little of the factory-produced aura of manufactured cool would cocoon them, seemed to have the exact opposite effect. They ran gleefully and drunkenly through the streets of Prague and it didn't seem to me like they were actually tasting freedom. It seemed like they were slumming it with the quotidian.

It is easy to put down Frances Trollope as a Tory embittered by her American business failure. But her observations on American manners, confirmed by many other observers foreign and domestic, actually provide a sharply drawn picture of daily life in the young republic. Most observers at the time agreed with her in finding Americans obsessively preoccupied with earning a living and relatively uninterested in leisure activities. Not only Tories but reformers like Martineau and Charles Dickens angered their hosts by complaining of the overwhelmingly commercial tone of American life, the worship of the "almighty dollar." Americans pursued success so avidly they seldom paused to smell the flowers. A kind of raw egotism, unsoftened by sociability, expressed itself in boastful men, demanding women, and loud children. The amiable arts of conversation and cooking were not well cultivated, foreigners complained; Tocqueville found American cuisine "the infancy of the art" and declared one

New York dinner he attended "complete barbarism." Despite their relatively broad distribution of prosperity, Americans seemed strangely restless; visitors interpreted the popularity of the rocking chair as one symptom of this restlessness. Another symptom, even more emphatically deplored, was the habit, widespread among males, of chewing tobacco and spitting on the floor. Women found their long dresses caught the spittle, which encouraged them to avoid male company at social events. Chewing tobacco thus reinforced the tendency toward social segregation of the sexes, with each gender talking among themselves about their occupations, the men, business and politics; the women, homemaking and children. Daniel Walker Howe, *What Hath God Wrought: The Transformation of America, 1815-1848*

Journalist Sebastian Junger, whose time spent embedded with troops in Afghanistan resulted in the award-winning film *Restrepo*, wrote a slim but powerful book about the problems soldiers and marines have in adjusting to civilian life after combat. The book isn't perfect. Junger's scathing critique of our contemporary world is mostly implicit, enmeshed so fully in the conversationally disarming tone of the book that you almost come away from it feeling soothed rather than rattled. It lists the symptoms we suffer in our anomic world, but never fully sinks its teeth into a critique of society. It never offers up solutions, political or social, that lie beyond the shrunken borders of mainstream American liberal consciousness. The book, which should feel dangerous, is too tame to fully address the issues that it involves itself with. It was written to be a bestseller, not to unsettle. Or in shooting range parlance, it aimed center mass. It isn't a head shot.

Nevertheless, it's an important book just by virtue of it suggesting that PTSD in vets and feelings of dislocation from society aren't solely caused by combat experiences, but that the problem might be with our society itself. Sure, our modern world is a kind of "paradise," Junger says, flush with technological innovation, relative safety and ease. His words are worth quoting at length here:

> The vast majority of us don't, personally, have to grow or kill our own food, build our own dwellings, or defend ourselves from wild animals and enemies. In one day we can travel a thousand miles by pushing down on a gas pedal or around the world by booking a seat on an airplane. When we are in pain we have narcotics that dull it out of existence, and when we are depressed we have pills that change the chemistry of our brains. We understand an enormous amount about the universe, from subatomic particles to our own bodies to galaxy clusters, and we use that knowledge to make life even better and easier for ourselves. The poorest people in modern society enjoy a level of physical comfort that was unimaginable a thousand years ago, and the wealthiest people live the way gods were imagined to have.
> And yet.

Pause and contemplate that "And yet" buried beneath the cavalcade of praise. You knew it was coming. You could feel the hollowness of his intentionally one-sided but absolutely factual veneration. There's a shadow that trails civilization. There's a price that we pay for what we gain in comfort and power, a price that we're usually so strongly dissuaded from contemplating that we hardly speak about it at all. And it eats away at us from the inside like a hidden secret. All that is contained in Junger's "And yet." He continues:

> There are many costs to modern society, starting with its toll on the global ecosystem and working one's way down to its toll on the human psyche, but the most dangerous cost may

be to community. If the human race is under threat in some way that we don't yet understand, it will probably be at a community level that we either solve the problem or fail to. If the future of the planet depends on, say, rationing water, communities of neighbors will be able to enforce new rules far more effectively than even local government. It's how we evolved to exist, and it obviously works.

I can't make the case that humans have evolved to exist in platoon-sized communities using scientific evidence and statistics. But I can say that my own experiences – not cold data, but the warm intimate crush of sweating and bleeding beside other men and knowing that we stand in debt to each other for each breath we draw – cohere with those of the veterans that Junger interviews. I've been rattled by the same confusion that follows a return home from war when you hear civilians contextualize your experience in political language. As if you had been fighting for your country and not your platoon and company. I've felt the heavy abstraction of patriotism laid against me as a critique. The anxious glances of people wondering why you participated in a defunct political cause. But you didn't, at least not in any way that feels connected to how you experienced the military. Love of country was there of course, like an ideal, and with the gauzy texture of a half-forgotten dream. But loyalty and experience arose from the tactile environment. The men filling sandbags with you. Their individual shapes and smells and laughter. And the knowledge that they, as my drill sergeant made explicit, would die for you.

And so it wasn't so much that patriotism was absent, but that it was shorn of abstraction and condensed into the familiarity of your platoon. A little America in a tent under a foreign sky.

The most obvious difference to my mind between civilian and military conceptions of "community" is in the understanding of what communities require in order to exist. Robert Nisbet defined the needs of a community as having: a purpose, transcendent dogma, definition of legitimate authority, a hierarchy, solidarity, sense of honor and a sense of innate superiority which separates them from outside So to say that these are all things that I miss about the military, things that are difficult to find in the contemporary civilian world (much less all in one place), is really most simply to say that I miss community.

The supermarket shelves have been rearranged. It happened one day without warning. There is agitation and panic in the aisles, dismay in the faces of older shoppers.[...]They scrutinize the small print on packages, wary of a second level of betrayal. The men scan for stamped dates, the women for ingredients. Many have trouble making out the words. Smeared print, ghost images. In the altered shelves, the ambient roar, in the plain and heartless fact of their decline, they try to work their way through confusion. But in the end it doesn't matter what they see or think they see. The terminals are equipped with holographic scanners, which decode the binary secret of every item, infallibly. This is the language of waves and radiation, or how the dead speak to the living. And this is where we wait together, regardless of our age, our carts stocked with brightly colored goods. A slowly moving line, satisfying, giving us time to glance at the tabloids in the racks. Everything we need that is not food or love is here in the tabloid racks. The tales of the supernatural and the extraterrestrial. The miracle vitamins, the cures for cancer, the remedies for obesity. The cults of the famous and the dead.
Don DeLillo, *White Noise*

Chapter 4

Hierarchy

Ichthyophils imagine that human beings want a life in which they can make their own choices. But what if they can be fulfilled only by a life in which they follow each other? The majority who obey the fashion of the day may be acting on a secret awareness that they lack the potential for a truly individual existence. Liberalism – the ichthyophil variety, at any rate – teaches that everyone yearns to be free. Herzen's experience of the abortive European revolutions of 1848 led him to doubt that this was so. It was because of his disillusionment that he criticized Mill so sharply. But if it is true that Mill was deluded in thinking that everyone loves freedom, it may also be true that without this illusion there would be still less freedom in the world. The charm of a liberal way of life is that it enables most people to renounce their freedom unknowingly.

John Gray, *The Silence of Animals: On Progress and Other Modern Myths*

Before I joined the military, the word "authority" had a bitterness to it. I remember riding passenger side in a relative's truck one summer night before I went off to basic training and him warning me that in the Army I would be told "when to shave, when to shit, and when to shower." Authority, all authority had certain associations with it: arbitrary, corrupt, harsh, brutal. For a kid obsessed with The Beats, the word "authority" seemed like an antonym to the word "legitimate." It was what happened when people with deep neuroses about their own strength and value imposed their will on others to, most often, nefarious ends.

The counterargument to this naive rendering is obvious. As

I heard someone say one day in Baghdad in 2007 while we were fortifying a combat outpost (COP), "You don't need leadership to get people to eat donuts." And you don't. But one obviously can't live off donuts alone. We also owe each other more than just donuts. We owe each other a certain amount of sacrifice that doesn't always naturally issue forth freely from us.

My memories of building the COP just south of the Baghdad International Airport aren't really a blur, as the cliche goes, but more of a series of still images, randomized and scattered throughout my mind. Filling sandbags with our sharp, black shovel-like Entrenchment Tools, or "E Tools." Cleaning the dark bathrooms of the building complex that we occupied with their dusty cracked blue tiles and center of the room drain which seemed like an old metal eye half-conscious, half-aware of our presence. Tower guard over-watching a new and unfamiliar part of the city that felt more overtly hostile than the neighborhoods we had previously patrolled. Eating MREs in a hallway, waiting for our turn to pull guard, making crass jokes and daydreaming about our future lives.

My memories exist in possessive plural because, of course, we were always together. But also because all of our activities were for each other. And this, I think, was at the heart of what I came to understand about leadership when it's at its best and functioning as it should: it exists to make certain that we exist for each other. The business of survival, especially in a war zone, isn't easy. It isn't eating donuts. And leadership, authority, is the method by which we most efficiently serve each other.

This aspect of authority tends to get lost in the more cartoonish popular renderings of it. And perhaps the most misunderstood symbol of military authority, the one which when properly understood reveals something almost astonishing at the center of martial authority, is the salute.

The origins of the military salute are too ancient to be discussed as anything except legend and myth. It could have started in Rome, where the right hand, or weapon-wielding hand, was ceremonially revealed to be empty when greeting a dignitary. It could have come about during the Middle Ages, with knights raising visors to reveal their identities. Most likely it arose long before either of these, as a peaceful symbol of deference and cooperation that seems almost synonymous with human culture itself. And it isn't simply European. The eighteenth century Shawnee warrior and chief Tecumseh said: "Always give a word or sign of salute when meeting or passing a friend, or even a stranger, if in a lonely place." The salute's profundity as a gesture often means that even today it retains an overt spiritual or religious aura. Think of the Sikh "Sat Sri Akai" greeting, with palms held together near the heart. Or what we experienced in Iraq, the traditional Arabic greeting of salaam with the right hand held against the heart. These examples and the many others from around the world and throughout time pierce to the core of what the salute represents: a recognition of our shared participation in the hierarchy of being and an acknowledgment of our fealty to each other.

The military salute is probably the ceremonial gesture most misunderstood by civilians. When an enlisted person salutes an officer, it shouldn't be taken as a sign of subservience or some brute artifact of force. What it's more akin to is a recognition of common purpose and of the fundamental unity that exists among the varied roles that each person plays in the larger nexus of the military community. A website called the Army Study Guide explains:

> The salute is not simply an honor exchanged. It is a privileged gesture of respect and trust among soldiers. Remember the salute is not only prescribed by regulation but is also recognition of each other's commitment, abilities, and professionalism...The salute is widely misunderstood outside the military. Some consider it to be a gesture of

servility since the junior extends a salute to the senior, but we know that it is quite the opposite. The salute is an expression that recognizes each other as a member of the profession of arms; that they have made a personal commitment of self-sacrifice to preserve our way of life. The fact that the junior extends the greeting first is merely a point of etiquette – a salute extended or returned makes the same statement.

A salute binds a vertical hierarchy together by reminding all parties of a common purpose. It isn't about subservience to force or obsequiousness toward a personality. As Jane MacDougall writes in *The National Post*:

> There are so many ways of communicating via gestures enshrined in tradition: the handshake, the tip of the hat — all intended as acts of friendship. None of the salutes imply obeisance; each is designed to convey respect. In the British tradition, a salute isn't for the individual but acknowledges the royal commission of the individual: it's the job, and not the person, who's being saluted. And the respect is always reciprocated with the salute being returned.

That the salute is always returned is important. Its reciprocal nature gestures toward an understanding of leadership, authority and hierarchy that often gets distorted by civilian rhetoric and values. Hierarchy, at its best and most ideal, isn't about arbitrary power but legitimate authority in the service of some collective goal. The salute indicates a recognition of this order and purpose. And what might seem to a civilian like a symbol of personal degradation is in truth a gesture of pride in the shared sacrifices and goals of every individual within the hierarchy itself.

How can one explain this trend towards a more colorless and

shallow life? Well, the work was easier, if less healthy, and it brought in more money, more leisure, and perhaps more entertainment. A day in the country is long and hard. And yet the fruits of their present life were worthless compared to a single coin of their former life: a rest in the evening and a rural festivity. That they no longer knew the old kind of happiness was obvious from the discontentment which spread over their features. Soon dissatisfaction, prevailing over all their other moods, became their religion.

Ernst Junger, *The Glass Bees*

Authority bonds us to each other in both senses of the word – it connects as it fetters. But just as the connections that authority promotes aren't necessarily always healthy or moral, the constraints of authority aren't necessarily always negative. Both in the right contexts and with the proper intentions are useful. Enjoyable, even.

In his book *Authority*, sociologist Richard Sennett explores our contemporary ambiguous relationship with the idea of authority. Whereas Classical literature tends to dramatize the break-down of authority, our contemporary fears are more about too readily admitting authority into our personal lives. We have a very real desire to live materially stable lives with as much convenience as possible, but we're afraid of false authority taking advantage of that and using our desires to constrain our freedom.

Sennett writes:

There are many ingredients of this modern fear [of authority]. In part it is a fear of the authorities as seducers. In part it is a fear of the act of seduction, of liberty yielding to security. In part it is a fear of the seduced, of the masses who might be weak-willed. Again, most figures of authority do not arouse much enthusiasm because they do not deserve to. An intelligent person remains sane by rejecting the childish collages of strength and compassion which the authorities present as pictures of themselves. Yet our rejection is not connected to our seeing a better image of authority in our mind's eye. And our need for authority as such remains. Desires for guidance, security, and stability do not disappear when they are unsatisfied.

Our fears of authority, the trepidation we feel toward the very real power that authority holds over us (a seductive power, as Sennett points out), comes in large part from a half-conscious realization that we desire authority. That it's necessary.

Fatherless now, you must deal with the memory of a father. Often that memory is more potent than the living presence of a father, is an inner voice commanding, haranguing, yes-ing and no-ing – a binary code, yes no yes no yes no yes no, governing your every, your slightest movement, mental or physical. At what point do you become yourself? Never, wholly, you are always partly him. That privileged position in your inner ear is his last "perk" and no father has ever passed it by.
Donald Barthelme, *The Dead Father*

Authority bonds and guides, but what is it exactly? We have a fairly intuitive sense of authority, but that same intuition is clouded by a lot of gauzy emotion and cultural effluvia surrounding the notion of power and its abuses. Here, Richard Sennett is helpful again. Before he became a sociologist, Sennett was studying to be a professional musician. And for Sennett, the supreme exemplar of authority at its best was the conductor Pierre Monteux. Lacking charisma or an overpowering dogmatic presence, Monteux nevertheless restricted his baton movements to a tiny imaginary box just a little larger than one foot by one foot. His minimalism of movement and lack of dramatic flair actually seemed to draw the orchestra in, tightly attuning them to even the most subtle movements and variations. His subdued body movements, a raise of the eyebrows or a glance, communicated more to an orchestra than the most overwrought gesticulations of other conductors.

Monteux's authority derived in large part from his calm sense of control. Sennett says that his "assurance was the cornerstone of his authoritativeness." When a leader is comfortable being in control, others are comfortable relinquishing to them. He didn't need to scream or stomp around in a lurid display of aggression in order to assert his authority. Sennett writes:

> There was no coercion, no threat; there was simply a man who was trying to help one be better. Better, that is to say, play what he wanted, for he knew. His aura was of one who had achieved an understanding that made it possible for him to judge in the most relaxed way. And this too is an essential ingredient in authority: someone who has strength and uses it to guide others through disciplining them, changing how they act by reference to a higher standard.

I can't think of a more apt description of authority within the military than that last sentence. It was generally known among young leaders (and in the military everyone is expected at some point and in some context to rise to the challenge of leadership) that to be constantly screaming at your subordinates, to feel backed into a position where you're constantly tormenting them, is the most tell-tale sign of weakness in a leader. It means that you've lost control. That your authority has been compromised. As Sennett says, guiding people by reference to a higher standard is the core of authority, but it's almost just as important that it be communicated in a calm, self-assured way. Half the task of authority is in helping people to understand, through a combination of mutual respect and trust, that you all share the same transcendent goals. You don't need leadership to eat donuts, and part of the task of legitimate authority is in convincing people that they deserve something more profound than a baker's dozen.

> Real leaders are people who help us overcome the limitations of our own individual laziness and selfishness and weakness and fear and get us to do better, harder things than we can get ourselves to do on our own.
>
> David Foster Wallace, *The Weasel, Twelve Monkeys and the Shrub*

To live in the modern world, to be here now and in this historical moment, is to have a knee-jerk distrust of any authority outside of the self. There's a strong argument that modernity began with a combination of Machiavelli's cold-eye gazing at the power machinations of the Borgias and Luther's resistance to Ecclesiastical authority. The warp and woof of our thoughts are at one with a radical individualism which guides us toward a profound and cynical suspicion of all authoritative limits. So it shouldn't come as a surprise that our strongest and most popular cultural representations of crises of authority sketch out nightmarish visions of overly strong and very nearly demonic leaders. And while it's true that literary figures like Captain Ahab or Cormac McCarthy's Judge Holden, conduits for violence and pain, serve transcendent ends – goals which appear to loom outside and above them and their followers but guide all of their actions – their maniacal focus and hypnotic energy only seems evil. Spiritual figures though they might be, they're petty tyrants. The philosophies directing them are really solipsism, power and obsession, themselves transformed into animating principles. Transcendence which only collapses back into itself.

They rode on. They rode like men invested with a purpose

whose origins were antecedent to them, like blood legatees of an order both imperative and remote. For although each man among them was discrete unto himself, conjoined they made a thing that had not been before and in that communal soul were wastes hardly reckonable more than those whited regions on old maps where monsters do live and where there is nothing other of the known world save conjectural winds.
Cormac McCarthy, *Blood Meridian*

Oliver Stone's 1986 film *Platoon* doesn't need an introduction as possibly the most well-known American anti-war film. Stone was there. He served in Vietnam. And so even though the film occasionally deals in cartoonish oversimplifications, it does capture something of the very real and very powerful bifurcations experienced in the military and perhaps in American society more generally. Most fundamentally, there are the civilians off screen versus the soldiers and Vietnamese civilians we see in the film. Then there are the Americans and the Vietnamese. And within the Americans themselves there are the drinkers versus the smokers: the sad, violent, mostly white contingent drinking and playing cards to a background of country music, whose style and ethos stands fundamentally opposed to the hash smokers, a multi-racial motley smiling and dancing to R&B.

The drinkers are solipsistic nihilists, just trying to kill. The smokers are escapists, just trying to survive. And each have their representative leaders. The drinkers have Staff Sergeant Barnes, cold, cruel and with a face etched by a wild topography of scars. He speaks and acts for power. Sergeant Elias, a gaunt Jesus figure who eventually dies for his moral code, is a figure of legitimate authority in the full sense of the word. Barnes serves murky chthonic forces that always fold back in on themselves. Death for death's sake. He eventually even murders Sergeant Elias, whose adherence to a transcendent morality, even in the context of a dubious colonizing war effort, interferes with Barnes' attempts to flatten and empty the world of moral value. In another context, you might call Barnes' quest the desacralization of the world.

Barnes versus Elias is a metaphor for the confrontation between misdirected power and legitimate authority, but what are the specifics of the struggle?

The word authority derives from the Latin *auctor*, which Richard Sennett says can refer to a guarantor of action. Something or someone imbued with the ability to make good on the promise that our actions will continue to have meaning and coherence through time. So, in some sense, true authority represents a defiance of the entropic ravages of time. A dam against nihilism. A bid for the continuity of coherence. Power on the other hand is force completely shorn of its own significance.

Sennett writes: "Of authority it may be said in the most general way that it is an attempt to interpret the conditions of power, to give the conditions of control and influence a meaning by defining an image of strength. The quest is for a strength that is solid, guaranteed, stable." But, Sennett warns, beware of thinking that you've finally settled on the final and perfect authority. The point is to endlessly search, to carve an arc through toward your Ithaca, without finally settling on anything permanent. I'm not so sure. In vaguely lauding the "search" for authority without clearly articulating any sort of hierarchy of values which would order the search or even articulate the significance of the search itself, any warning against coming into port itself conceals a kind of power. What is this power? It's the same power that I felt fill my days and hours as a civilian after my time in the Army. The soft nihilism of making a fetish of choice itself, which can end in its own forms of petty tyranny of the self over the self.

The tyranny of the leader obsessed with the uncertainty of their own authority, so often filled as it is with the Nietzschean *ressentiment* of the unorthodox, can become sublimely grim. With their power and insecurity comingled, a macabre sort of alloy is synthesized. The most obvious examples of this are found in smaller people, physically diminutive and socially either ostracized or cut off from traditional modes of authority. Charles Manson is probably the most notorious example of this kind of bad underdog leader of broken people. Maybe their cause is at least partially valid. Maybe they're justified in feeling a sort of righteous indignation. But if that moral umbrage and transcendence of purpose gets folded back in on itself, if the focus becomes simply revenge or a compulsive picking at existential scabs, it then becomes an infinite regression of anger and pain still somehow resonating with, and emboldened by, the dead echo of moral virtue.

The most terrifying nihilistic petty tyrants are children. Not only do they represent a perfect confluence of physical and social powerlessness, but their egoism hasn't yet been tempered by larger social institutions. They're outsiders and they feel it. They don't yet seem perfectly enmeshed into the world. Their experiences haven't yet had time to humble them. Yukio Mishima wrote perhaps the most disturbing novel about the nihilistic authority of petty tyranny with his slim masterpiece *The Sailor Who Fell from Grace with the Sea*. We're comfortable interpreting the story about a band of murderous although otherwise quite normal (well, for the most part) Japanese school children as an allegory for Japanese anxiety toward American cultural influence, but there's also a darker and more obvious reading available to us. The novel can be read, more disturbingly and rewardingly, as an expose of sick authority.

The novel focuses mostly on the actions of Noburu Kuroda, a schoolboy living in Yokohama whose widow mother falls in love with a sailor. Noburu runs with a strange cultish group of young nihilists led by a boy called "chief." When the romantic figure of a sailor called Ryuji Tsukazaki becomes romantically involved with Noburu's mother and decides to give up his life at sea for the domesticity of Yokohama, the children decide to murder

Ryuji for giving up his maritime heroism for domestic order. In deciding to kill Ryuji, chief gives a speech that reverberates with the resentment of someone aware of their own power but not yet able to understand the more complex nature of its relation to authority:

There is no such thing as a good father because the role itself is bad. Strict fathers, soft fathers, nice moderate fathers – one's as bad as another. They stand in the way of our progress while they try to burden us with their inferiority complexes, and their unrealized aspirations, and their resentments, and their ideals, and the weaknesses they've never told anyone about, and their sins, and their sweeter-than-honey dreams, and the maxims they've never had the courage to live by – they'd like to unload all this silly crap on us, all of it! Even the most neglectful fathers, like mine, are no different. Their consciences hurt them because they've never paid attention to their children and they want the kids to understand just how bad the pain is – to sympathize!

On New Year's Day we went to Arashi Yama in Kyoto and as we were crossing the Bridge of Moons I asked my old man a question: "Dad, is there any purpose in life?" You see what I was getting at, don't you, what I really meant? Father, can you give me one single reason why you go on living? Wouldn't it be better just to fade away as quickly as possible? But a first class insinuation never reaches a man like that. He just looked surprised and his eyes bugged out and he stared at me. I hate that kind of ridiculous adult surprise. And when he finally answered, what do you think he said? "Son, nobody is going to provide you with a purpose in life; you've got to make one for yourself."

How's that for a stupid, hackneyed moral!

It would be disingenuous of me to say that there weren't any of

Mishima's chiefs in the Army. There were. There were all kinds of distortions of what true leadership should be. There were, in fact, archetypes of bad leaders. Low rent versions of Captain Ahab, men twisted by strange personal rancor from their pasts who carried their bitterness to the job and then elevated it to an almost metaphysical grandeur. There were Judge Holdens, inscrutable in their vacuous cruelty. But there were leaders who failed in the opposite direction, as it were. Timid and pliant, unable to take a stand for the men serving under them. People defined by their insecurity, who cared more about feeling like friends with their subordinates than in fealty to their responsibilities as leaders. In many cases, the ones who wanted to be your friend were even more dangerous than the hardened sadistic ones, because that friendship really only moved in one direction, only benefited them. It was a kind of moral laziness. They felt uncomfortable making demands of you, and then would throw you under the bus the instant that their own superior came down on them. It wasn't kindness. It was their path of least resistance.

My grandmother is a Tarot card reader. And, having been close to her from birth, I learned to read Tarot cards before I learned to read English. So when I think associatively about authority, my mind moves to the visual dichotomy between The Hierophant card and The Devil card. In the Rider-Waite deck the images of the two figures echo each other. They appear as two forces moving in opposite directions while remaining joined at a common fixed point of origin. Both are seated on thrones positioned above acolytes. Each has their right hand raised and forming a symbolic gesture. In their left hands they each hold some sort of staff. In the case of the hierophant it's an elegant gold crosier. The Devil holds a flaming torch. They look similar, even sharing a placid expression of someone absolutely comfortable being in a hierarchical position.

But if the similarities are striking, the differences are even more so. The hierophant's crosier is made of gold, the most mystical mineral, and points up, as do his (or her? The figure is androgynous) middle and index fingers, which are held in the sign of benediction. The hierophant's followers are depicted only by the back of their heads, hair shaved into a Roman tonsure. Their authority and guidance comes from the hierophant, whose own authority and guidance comes from "above." What we see when we look at the card is something like an electrical circuit moving through each of the figures, and ourselves, channeling the energy of a higher authority.

The Devil meanwhile points down with his torch. His hand is held aloft with each finger extended and palm flattened. His acolytes are prisoners, not students, each chained to the column throne that he's perched upon. All three figures stare out at us almost antagonistically. This card is a depiction of power, not authority. There is no transcendent purpose, just the fire and wood of the torch pointing to the ground, the eternal loop of a specific moment and particular place. The followers are prisoners, chained not only to the dark throne, but to their own ego as expressed in their faces. They're cut off from anything higher than their own identities. They're prisoners to themselves.

In Alejandro Jodorowsky's idiosyncratic *The Way of the Tarot: The Spiritual Teacher in the Cards*, the filmmaker and amateur occultist has each of the major arcana speak in their own voices. The hierophant, or The Pope, as he's called in the Marseilles deck which Jodorowsky uses, says:

Within me is the same order found in the universe. I am an empty, shapeless vessel that transports the light wherever the wind wills. I place myself between Heaven and Earth, I urge its inhabitants with the hope of raising themselves to where there are no longer any limits. To everything that is rooted in matter or mind, I communicate the higher power that gives life to what is inanimate. It is through me that the flesh ascends to mind in sublime fireworks. It is through me that the flock of angelic energies descends toward the coldness of matter to dissolve into waves of magnetic heat.

I repulse all curses. I bless everything I hear, everything I see, everything I sense. I summon love like a bird to a dimension beyond measure, so that it may perch upon the smallness of a heart. What can I do about your family squabbles, your hardships, your wounds? I make them kneel down before me and pray. Let me come into you: I will bless your entire world, including your problems.

I invest all actions with my mission, awaken to the strength of the sacred. The least of your gestures, the least of your actions will then become sacred in turn. You will know the experience of one who does not speak his own name.

The cross in my hand is not an instrument for giving orders. It is the symbol of my joyful annihilation. I have pacified my desires, transformed the pack of ravenous wolves into a flock of swallows celebrating dawn with their song. I have turned the tumultuous ocean that agitated my heart into a lake of milk, as calm and sweet as that which flows from the breast of the Virgin. Whoever has my thirst may come drink from my spirit. I refuse nobody anything. I am the door that all keys may open.

Jodorowsky's Pope is poetic and strange. He doesn't just represent a conduit to some higher order, but also expresses the sweetness, clarity and creative potential of positive authority. It's an authority that has transcended dry legalisms and entered fully into its own splendor. There's more to good authority than an efficient utilitarianism. There's more phenomenological heft to the experience of serving under a good leader than the dry mechanics of how-to leadership books suggest. The whole of the experience is more than the sum of the parts. There's a certain sweetness to dignified authority, to working and existing within its field of influence, that doesn't properly have a name in our liquid world of delusional self-authorship.

I should know. It's my instinct to resist authority, an instinct that's occasionally rewarded in the civilian world but obviously isn't looked kindly upon in the military. My insubordination was more passive aggressive than anything. Not long after I showed up to my first permanent duty station near a small town in southern Germany, I skipped out on the mandatory driving classes (my rationale, if you want to call it that, was that driving is even easier in Europe than in America, with the signs intentionally created in a symbolic grammar that avoided written language – it all just seemed intuitive) and instead hung out in the base library. I was found out, busted down in rank and put on extra duty.

It wouldn't be the last time I was given an "Article 15" as they call it, a sort of in-house administrative punishment for actions that fall far short of being worthy of actual court action. If Article 15s were given in the civilian world, they'd fall somewhere between a traffic ticket and spending the night in jail. I also got in trouble for not immediately contacting my unit when I arrived at Baghdad International Airport after returning from leave. My reasoning this time was that they had my schedule, they knew I was there, and so I'd just wait for them to put my name on a helicopter manifest to return to my forward operating base. Instead, I was picked up by a convoy a few days later. I still maintain that this one wasn't entirely my fault.

My point is that I don't naturally take to authority. I'm proud, and stubbornly hard headed. And I didn't join the Army out of some desperate search for authority in my life, at least it wasn't a longing that I consciously had. So, when I say that good leadership, authentic authority, has a sort of existential sweetness to it, it isn't an admission that's made very easily. I don't think I would have made it while I was in the Army, even. But when I'm in my most confessional mode, it's an experience that I'm forced to admit having. There's a freedom in good authority. It isn't the kind of freedom you would find in coloring outside the lines or kicking over trash cans or staying in bed for weeks. When it's at its best, it's the kind of freedom you hear in a transcendent jazz solo or that you see in someone making a 3-point shot. It's the freedom of coming completely into your telos, of operating within your purpose at the highest level. It's the freedom of The Hierophant's acolytes completing a circuit with a higher order.

> A constant order of battle, a constant formation of advanced guards and outposts, are methods by which a general ties not only his subordinates' hands, but his own in certain cases.
> Von Clausewitz, *On War*

One of the ways to experience authority at its best is as a bonding or connection. Hierarchy is a community. A vertical community. So much in what poet Robert Bly calls our Sibling Society, in his book of the same name, has been flattened horizontally. He writes:

> Clouds form on the horizon [and] consumer goods roll in like fog or rain; people have little "interiority," as the Europeans say; instead we experience daily the rising tide of communication devices. Lively students hit an iceberg disguised as the public school, and French rafts cannot save them anymore. Because information pours in from all sides, we have little attention left for symbols.
>
> The average age of the advertising executives in say, McCann-Erikson, is not 34 or so. As in television, movies, the music business, advertising is run by the young for the young and almost no older mentors are left. The deepening and heightening of the psyche that was the distinctive virtue of older men and women is not a part of the sibling-driven corporation. The increasingly hurried and harried college

education that comes before business means that many men and women graduate without ever having any experience of the "other worlds" or of deeper meanings.

What Bly describes is a world completely denuded of, not just depth, but a hierarchy by which one accesses that depth. A world without established communities forming conduits to truths that contain more profundity than self-pleasure. More than simply eating donuts.

Bly goes on to write in *The Sibling Society*:

Christo art projects, detective stories, Disneylands, Madonna-like singers, Muzak, disco music, Hollywood movies, and that water running under the bridges of Madison County carry a certain single-minded optimism that fits with the excitement of aimless murder and aimless art, making a sideways view that leaves out all drowning. The influence of popular art is so great that many human beings now live their whole lives without meeting vertical attention in any embodiment that makes it feel real.

Vertical attention implies that ability, or at least the longing, to look downward; or the ability to look upward, at the stars, at the energies beyond the stars, at angels. One problem with the sibling society is that, in its intense desire to get away from hierarchy, it unintentionally avoids all vertical longing.

I'm not so convinced that the avoidance of all vertical longing in contemporary society is so unintentional, but Bly describes a tragically familiar world flattened by vapid consumerism and resonating with the empty promises of an equally vapid individualism. If hierarchy binds us together, it also, when it functions properly (a big when), helps us to cohere to one another in a real community, it also binds us in an equally profound way:

hierarchy resists ephemeral boundaries. The chain of command exists here and now, but the shape of hierarchy moves in three dimensions, breaks through our temporal isolation, and binds a community across time.

Chapter 5

Smoking

Cigarettes and war are synonymous. In fact, there's an apocryphal story about how the first cigarette was created in the nineteenth century when a Turkish soldier broke his pipe during combat and was forced to wrap his tobacco inside the paper of an empty cartridge shell. It's obviously inaccurate, since cigarette factories already existed in Spain during the first half of the century. Even so, as Richard Klein points out in his magisterial work *Cigarettes Are Sublime*, from the very beginning cigarettes had a dual association with both the military and bohemianism. Read the libretto for *Carmen*, the opera that Nietzsche called the best example of French operatic work, a work fated to outlive all others, and you'll be reading not only the first literary representation of a woman smoking, but also a sort of erotic struggle between the eponymous gypsy and her violent dragoon. The two opposed yet complementary energies that the cigarette is symbolic of, loving each other to death. Fated to join each other in the ash of this world as the final red glow of their passion burns out.

Why does the cigarette belong to the soldier? Why does the cigarette seem so suited to war? In some ways, the soldier resembles a cigarette. Each is uniform, visual similar. Both cigarettes and soldiers present themselves to the public in an orderly phalanx redolent of mechanical organization and factory-floor discipline. But behind the scenes, or behind the lines rather, soldiers and cigarettes can be found lounging in the disordered languidity of their own breath, the smoke of the cigarette mixing with the idle chatter of the soldier. The bodies of cigarettes soggy, bent and crushed in the pockets of soldiers who come to physically resemble their almost talismanic objects as combat wears on.

But the soldier and cigarette also resemble each other in a much more fundamental way: in their relation to time. If soldiers smoke out of boredom, to kill time, then the cigarettes they hold burning between their fingers also parallel the ephemerality of the soldier's existence. The tiny violence of the initial flame, the brief enjoyable interlude and then the extinguishing of the flame, snubbed out on the side of a tank or beneath a boot. The cigarette then is like a miniature version of the soldier, sacrificing its brief life for his temporary pleasure. But in that tiny sacrifice of paper and tobacco, is time really being killed? Do soldiers smoke as simply just something to do in the larger boredom of war, or is a more temporally complicated event happening?

When I lit a cigarette in Iraq, I wasn't smoking just to occupy time, but to transcend it. Or reconnect myself to it in a more substantial way. The duration of my smoke was a few minutes in a parallel existence, something beside or above the war itself, in which the smoke moving through my lungs connected me simultaneously to my own family history and the mostly absent fruits of civilization. Smoking is a kind of time travel.

For me, the travel isn't just an abstract transcendence of war time. It isn't only vertical travel. It also moves me backward through time to my own childhood. Each of my grandparents smoked (though my maternal grandmother eventually quit after a car accident), and so some of my earliest and warmest memories occurred in rooms with thick shag carpeting absorbing the smoke of multiple lit cigarettes. Older people sitting at tables with their wrists and ankles crossed, lightly tapping ash into brass trays. A few uncles and aunts smoking also, sometimes outside while youngsters pedaled Big Wheels down cracked and overgrown sidewalks. My Grandpa Joe with a hard pack of cigarettes in his flannel shirt pocket. Years later, when I would put a pack in my own pocket, the pressure of the rectangle against my chest made it so it felt like I was still hugging him goodbye.

My grandparents smoked. My parents hated smoking. They saw firsthand the ravages of smoking on the body. And to some extent, I did too. But the association of smoking with death would become a familiar and even reassuring presence to me that would echo both forward and backward through my life. The first dead body I ever saw was my Grandpa Joe's when I was 9 years old. He'd started smoking when he was young. Very young. During World War II he'd inhaled enough toxic fumes as a ball-turret gunner over the Pacific that he had to have a lung removed when the war ended. But he continued to smoke regardless, smoking not being a rational or utilitarian pursuit. And so when he eventually died of emphysema in the 90s, my mother brought me into his hospital room, his contorted body still punctured with tubes like a high-tech St Sebastian, to show me firsthand the grim physical consequences of smoking.

Years later in Iraq I would see my first corpse. It was at the end of a dusty street in a neighborhood in West Rashid, Baghdad. A small parade of laughing children had surrounded our patrol and led us, pointing and asking for chocolate, to the mutilated corpse. When they reached it, they joyfully formed a circled around it and waited for us to reward them with a soccer ball. Their parents stood smoking in doorways. The body itself, bloated from the sun, was bound and blindfolded. He had been tortured. Singed fat coagulated in drill holes. Cigarette burns spotted its mottled skin. Sitting behind a machine gun in a Humvee turret, I lit a cigarette myself and stepped both above and fully into the moment. Cigarettes had played a role in this death too. But the survivors, the neighborhood adults, me and a few other soldiers, also steeled ourselves against the finality of the violence by completing with our cigarette smoke a circuit that included, not only each other in our bodies on this half-ruined street in Baghdad, but our past and future lives as well. There is a reason that tobacco was worshiped as a deity in some native North American tribes, as a miniature god of compact, communion and time outside of time. And in these epiphanic moments of cigarette smoking, I understood that the power and reality of all these things – time, cigarettes, war – were more elusive than the bland utilitarians back home would have me believe. That the smoking didn't kill us or sustain us, but instead fostered something more like an attitude toward life. A position from which to see things. A soot through which ineffable connections could be experienced firsthand.

Cigarettes fill the gap where the horseshoe ends of culture almost touch. Who smokes? Working-class people with rough hands and tattoos. Blue-collar workers on smoke breaks beside strip mall dumpsters or on construction sites. The cigarette an extension of earthiness, as in my own family. The cigarette box at once another colorful consumer product comparable to a cereal box, each with its own distinguishable font and coloring and market-tested identity, but also a panoply of elemental ingredients weighting the consumer to the Earth: paper, vegetation, fire, smoke. The cigarette is (or was, at least) a symbol of American working-class identity. Alienated in their toil, whether on a desolate rural plain or the hot innards of an urban factory, smoking becomes almost a way of communing with oneself. A secular ceremony celebrating the sensuality of people whose desires usually come as an afterthought, if at all, to the larger society.

But if smoking belongs to the trailer parks and union halls, it has an equal claim placed upon it by the elegant, the bohemian artist or dandy. If on one end of the spectrum smoking is succor for the physical laborer, it's equally reverenced on the other by those who either don't work at all or whose work is purely creative or mental. Baudelaire reminds us that in breathing the smoke of the cigarette into our lungs and letting it mingle with our innards on a cellular level before releasing it back into the world, smoking mirrors the poetic process of the artist inhaling the world and retreating back into a vibrant self-regard. Klein writes in *Cigarettes Are Sublime*:

> In Baudelaire's mythology, the worldly figure of poetic
> experience who best embodies these two impulses
> simultaneously, is the dandy...A continuous self-invention,
> the dandy is both ruthlessly rigorous and infinitely ephemeral,
> the subjective correlative of a sonnet's mathematical effusions,
> or of the meticulously repeated satisfactions of a cigarette. The
> aesthetic religion of lyric dandyism, the morality of making
> a work of art out of a way of life, finds its most precious relic
> in the cigarette, whose invention roughly coincided, in 1830,
> of the Parnassian dandy, who called himself Art and whose
> doctrine was "Art for Art's sake."

The two smokers, the worker and the dandy, blend in my
own experiences and imagination in the image of the Beatnik.
Specifically Kerouac. If the air of my grandparents' homes was
marbled with gray smoke from perpetually lit cigarettes, and
the bookshelves in my own room were filled with adventure
classics – *The Three Musketeers*, *Treasure Island*, *Tom Sawyer* – then
in Kerouac's work I found as a teenager the perfect admixture
of aesthetic adventurism and the familiar emotional weight of
familial love. It wasn't art for art's sake, nor was it a mute and
expressionless physicality, but a combination of the best of both
to synthesize something truly exciting: a spiritual literature that
sanctified the material world. Of course, I started off in the place
every teenager starts off with Kerouac, in reading *On the Road*,
but what interested me most about his work wasn't what some
people categorize as hedonism, but the exact opposite. What
appealed to me most was the headlong rush into experiential
meaning itself. The richness that ephemerality brings to life. The
mysteries of joy. The knowledge of eternity. As Benedict Giamo
writes in *Kerouac, the Word and the Way: Prose Artist as Spiritual
Quester*:

As a modernist mystic, Kerouac believed that direct knowledge of God, spiritual truth, and ultimate reality could be attained through subjective experience (conceived as intuition or insight). This was both his wager and means for being intoxicated – drunk with life – (helped along, as always, by alcohol and/or drugs). His aim, however, was not to get smashed; rather it was to get a higher purchase on the ecstasy of being in order to forge mystical bond with the divine or ultimate.

And to me, most of his spiritual/literary success came with the tiny, compact little spiritual tracts dedicated to the loss of specific people: *Tristessa*, *Visions of Gerard*, *Maggie Cassidy*. Each figure flickers like a votive candle in Kerouac's life, as transitory as the cigarettes constantly burning in his hands, sacralized by their ephemerality. Kerouac's devotion to our brief moments of love and chaos on the Earth provide the coordinates to where consciousness and material existence intersect so intimately that a tiny dot of eternity shines through the sublunary world. But only momentarily, of course. The star blinks out. The cigarette cherry grays into cool ash.

In war, cigarettes serve a similar albeit more secular function to Kerouac's tiny glowing eternity. They unstick us from the miasma of time and give us, if not control over it, then at least a moment of detached perspective. And like Kerouac's cigarettes blending in my mind (in my physical body as well) the intimacy of the tactile with the bohemian headiness of the aesthetic, cigarettes in war project us further into the physical immediacy of the moment while also reconnecting us with civilization.

In war you smoke to stay awake. You smoke because you're tired. You smoke because you're in pain. You smoke because you're afraid. You smoke because you're bored. If the nineteenth-century military emphasis on logistics can be summed up by Napoleon's aphorism that an army moves on its stomach, then war in the twentieth century (and the beginning of the twenty-first, at least for now) should be associated with General Pershing's letter to the Minister of War during World War I: "You ask what will win this war. I will tell you, we need tobacco, more tobacco – even more than food."

Cigarettes both signify and induce bravery. They steel a soldier against death and suffering while also being emblematic of a flamboyant haughtiness in the face of mortality. They produce their own jaunty courage. And not only for soldiers. Even prisoners condemned to death are traditionally allowed the right to a final cigarette. One last puff before the hood is placed over their heads. The most famous historical instance of a condemned prisoner drawing courage in their final moments from a puff of tobacco is the execution of Sir Walter Raleigh by King James I on erroneous charges of treason. Richard Klein writes of Raleigh, "that noble privateer who plagued the Spanish Main, the man who introduced Virginia tobacco to England, the gallant favorite of James' hated predecessor, a symbol of the new pleasures and perspectives that the Elizabethan age had brought to the dour religious perspectives of sixteenth-century England." Still smoking his pipe, Raleigh walked across the platform toward the chopping block, picked up the axe and said: "This is sharp medicine, but it will cure all disease," before he was decapitated with pipe still in mouth.

If smoking is a sort of amulet against death, it's also an invitation to communion. Among prisoners and soldiers there can exist an informal economy based on the trade of tobacco for food, favors and a blind eye. In Erich Remarque's *All Quiet on the Western Front*, cigarettes become cash for bribes:

"But aren't you authorized to give them morphine injections?..."

I put in his hand another couple of cigarettes: "Listen, do this to be nice..."

"OK," he said.

I had a policy myself, shared by most of the other soldiers I knew who smoked (because not all did, especially not all officers), that when I was deployed "down range" in Iraq I always bummed out a cigarette to anyone who asked. Because if cigarettes were a kind of currency, they had equal claim to being a universal bonding agent. Tokens of comradery that we owed each other out of respect for our mutual experience. And giving another soldier a cigarette was almost a non-hierarchical salute. A lateral recognition of being stuck all together in the same circumstances and working toward the same ends. Hemingway captures this smoking bond in *For Whom The Bell Tolls* when he writes:

"There is food soon," he said. "Do you have tobacco?"

Robert Jordan went over to the packs and opening one, felt inside an inner pocket and brought out one of the flat boxes of Russian cigarettes he had gotten at Golz's headquarters. He ran his thumbnail around the edge of the box and, opening the lid, handed them to Pablo who took half a dozen. Pablo, holding them in one of his huge hands, picked one up and looked at it against the light. They were long narrow cigarettes with pasteboard cylinders for mouthpieces.

"Much air and little tobacco," he said. "I know these. The other with the rare name had them."

"Kashkin," Robert Jordan said and offered the cigarettes to the gypsy and Anselmo, who each took one.

"Take more," he said and they each took another. He gave them each four more, they making a double nod with the hand holding the cigarettes so that the cigarette dipped its end as a man salutes with a sword, to thank him.

Cigarettes are used to face death and to acknowledge interdependence. But it can't be denied that they're also smoked to steel oneself against killing, most commonly after the act itself, and for the same reason that they're smoked to resist boredom or to calm an existential sense of danger: to elevate a part of oneself above the frenetic stickiness of the moment. Maybe that's the same reason why the executioner doesn't share a cigarette with the condemned. Not wanting to commune with the prisoner in an elevated tobacco-induced moment outside of time where he can see the condemned's face clearly in their shared nest of smoke, he instead smokes after the moment of death, when the head has rolled or the body slumped to the ground. Sir Walter Raleigh's pipe rolls to the ground and through his hood the executioner lights his own.

If cigarettes symbolize the elemental – fire, air and vegetation – then the communion they offer soldiers is rooted in the chthonic. Sharing a smoke is sharing breath. But it's also distribution of harvested plant, lit with a Promethean fire which in its controlled use reenacts the mythic foundations of human society with each flick of the lighter. Cigarettes are simultaneously primordial and representative of the highest achievement of civilization.

I don't remember what I smoked before I went to my permanent duty station in a small town in Germany. But I do remember what I smoked after I got there. Gauloises. The bright blue box with the white winged helmet on the front. Historically French but produced and sold in Germany. First released to the general public at the turn of last century, on the precipice of World War I, the blue of the Gauloises packaging, the bleu des Vosges and the patriotic blue of the French infantryman was and perhaps still is the perfect symbol of pride in Gallic culture. Though I was stationed in Germany, smoking Gauloises felt like the most visceral way for me to connect to the cultural depth that had been missing from my American suburban upbringing. Smoking Gauloises while walking through the Munich Altstadt, dizzy with tobacco and in a culture-induced fugue state, I felt myself like an infantryman in another sense. I felt like someone eager to enlist in the battle to reorient myself toward a cultural tradition. A bohemian foot soldier. The list of famous artists who smoked Gauloises was like a phalanx: John Lennon, Pablo Picasso, Henri Charrière, Sartre, Camus, Ravel, Nick Drake. And in joining them I was intentionally signaling my association with other Americans, such as Robert Motherwell, who understood the power of the Gauloises as symbol and icon. Motherwell smoked Lucky Strikes, Bernard Jacobson writes in the introduction to *Robert Motherwell, The Making of an American Giant*, "...but in his collage life he smokes Gauloises, around whose blue packets he now organizes one composition after another." Jacobson recognizes Motherwell using the Gauloises blue to quote, as it were, the history of French art, "by incorporating Gauloises packets he makes a deft and condensed allusion to 'French blue': to the Mediterranean and the palette of Matisse...to the smoke coiling up in a Cubist assemblage."

Gauloises were hard to come by in Iraq, so I switched to Newports, American and urban, their green packs having a cool and minimalist design so redolent of a mid-century vision of technological and social promise which was never quite achieved. The post-war dreams of American abundance collapsed into a consumerist caricature of itself. An almost sarcastic cigarette, of course, with sarcasm itself being one of the crowning achievements of civilization. This is what the cigarette keeps the soldier tethered to. It unifies the elemental and the abstract.

Cigarettes aren't like pipes or cigars or hand rolled joints. Where the cigar appears entirely organic, and the pipe more like a small household appliance than anything natural, the cigarette itself is the polished end result of a perfected manufacturing process. Within the brand and make, each cigarette is an exact replica of another. Each is neat and clean, anchored to a tight little filter and almost dapper in its thin suit of paper. In my gorilla box at the end of my bunk in Iraq was a small portable library of books ordered online and shipped to me overseas into a war zone via a global logistics supply chain as elegant and complex as it is decadent and wasteful. The cigarettes move via a similar route. Wrapped in their dapper paper and organized in their colorfully designed boxes, they were almost like a second library beside the books. Each smoke a page disappeared, a thought consumed. Composed of a plant cultivated in the Western Hemisphere, perfected in an industrial process equal parts Manchester and Detroit, and moved across the Earth by a series of logistical innovations comparable to an updated version of the Roman road system, the cigarette is a pleasure made possible to me by modernity. As Pierre Louÿs suggested in his short story "Une volupté nouevlle," when the ghost of a long-deceased Alexandrian woman appears on the protagonist's doorstep to measure and weigh the pleasures of the modern world, cigarettes are the only worthwhile indulgence that the Classical world didn't know. The only truly magnificent sensual delight that's been created since the fall of the Roman Empire.

Cigarettes are sensual, and a pleasure, but they're also gross. They're not something that appeals naturally to people, but are more of an acquired taste. Imagine the young kid trying a cigarette for the first time with friends, coughing and hacking, appalled at how something so coveted and addicting could have such a repulsive taste. The pleasures of smoking are more complicated than the joy of eating ice cream or even the mysteries of intoxication. The gratifications of cigarettes aren't obvious. To an external witness, the smoker may appear to simply be feeding an addiction. The act is no more sophisticated than scratching an itch, except that it's also colored with the moral failings of gluttonous self-harm. But more is happening with the smoker than meets the eye. We turn to Klein again, who writes:

> ...the physiological effect of nicotine has two stages. It not only raises blood pressure and pulse at the price of increasing discomfort – in the next moment it lowers them, producing

a marked feeling of release and relief. After mastering anxiety by increasing it, by giving it a precise, punctual origin, at the cost of more intense displeasure the organism that has taken a puff of its cigarette gets a little reward for its heroism: the sudden burst of unease that accompanies the ingestion of the poison is followed by a moment of release as the organism relaxes the tension that the poison, now eliminated, had initially provoked. The distension of the vessels and the slowing of the heart create a feeling of relaxation after the body's exertion in eliminating the toxin and combating its symptoms. From a psychological point of view the contradictory effects, like those of the Kantian sublime, paradoxically reinforce each other: less ease is the condition of more ease.

What Klein alludes to is the paradoxical nature of cigarettes as both harbingers of death and signifiers of the essence of what it means to be alive. Once again, we have the cigarette's metaphysical meaning curved into the shape of an ouroboros, joined at opposing ends. Vegetation joined with thought. Ephemerality tethered to the weight of the present moment. Solitary reverie with communal exchange. And we also have death, the physical reality of death in the form of a tumor, conjoined with the loftiest ideal of what it means to live.

The cigarette may go down in official reports as your cause of death, but it may also be a way of asserting some amount of ownership over your final end. In *Beyond the Pleasure Principle*, Freud writes of the idea of a natural death that:

We built up further conclusions on the basis of the assumption that all life must die from internal causes. We made this assumption so light-heartedly because it does not seem to us to be one. We are accustomed so to think, and every poet encourages us in the idea. Perhaps we have resolved so to think because there lies a certain consolation in this belief. If a man must himself die, after first losing his most beloved ones by death, he would prefer that his life be forfeit to an inexorable law of nature, a sublime Ανάχη, than to a mere accident which could have in some way been avoided. But perhaps this belief in the incidence of death as the necessary consequence of an inner law of being is also only one of those illusions we have fashioned for ourselves "so as to bear the burden of existence." It is certainly not a primordial belief: the idea of a "natural death" is alien to primitive races; they ascribe every death occurring among themselves to the influence of an enemy or an evil spirit.

We prefer, Freud tells us, the repetitive patterns we make for ourselves and the bushwhacking of our own personal path to death than submission to the blank and ineffable mysteries of fate. With every cigarette we partition off the vast realm of death's mysterious power and assert our own tiny bit of authorship over ourselves.

Freud wasn't of course the only heavyweight thinker to muse on smoking as a hedge against chaos in all its forms. Heidegger wrote in *Being and Time* that cigarettes can act as amulets against anxiety, as "Anxiety does not 'know' what is that in face of which it is anxious." And so cigarettes, with their nastiness and alarming physical effects, focus the mind on actual suffering, albeit in tiny and easily controlled doses. They create a "constant tranquilization about death." Hence the soldier who smokes before combat. The doomed prisoner's last cigarette. Sir Walter Raleigh's calm demeanor as he approached the axe.

Death. Anxiety. Courage. Soldiers. Philosophers. Such a unity of thought and being collated in the cigarette. In my own mind I associate the cigarette with the major arcana Tarot card The Magician. In the Rider-Waite deck the robed magician holds aloft in his right hand a candle burning at both ends. His left points to the ground. On a table before him are symbols of each of the suits of the Tarot deck: swords, cups, pentacles and wands. Flowers billow like fire from the bottom of the card. An infinity sign hangs over the magician's head. To me, this has always been the perfect symbol of the smoking artist, the creator combining all elements together and manipulating the effects of the material world according to some transcendent order which he channels through body and mind. Is it simply coincidence that the candle burning in his right hand resembles a cigarette?

The smoke from the magician's right hand, a familiar image from my grandmother's deck of Tarot cards, mingles with the smoke of Heidegger and Freud. Picasso's lit cigarette is mirrored in the glowing cherries of shell-shocked Iraqis, all sharing a common hunger to both transcend the moment and exert some existential control, no matter how small, over their own lives. Sir Walter Raleigh's head rolls away with a pipe still clenched between his dead teeth. An Iraqi who was tortured to death is riddled with cigarette burns. My grandfather's body stiff in the hospital, his alveoli worn to collapse like the Baghdad skyline. Each event, each person and each thought connected by a thin strand of smoke.

The first serious short story I tried to write was about my family. Thanksgiving in a house in rural Missouri and a long thin wisp of cigarette smoke coiled like a translucent serpent moving between rooms. Follow the smoke from one person to another. Past my laughing aunt flicking her long, skinny cigarette into a heavy glass ash tray. Into the hallway where a bearded uncle anxiously waits for someone to leave the bathroom. Into the living room where a grandpa falls asleep with a butt precariously balanced on top of a beer can. Now follow the smoke not only through physical space but through time as well. Entire generations connected by a pungent ash. Decades marked off in cartons of time.

But the story always failed somehow. Or, really, I failed it, because I didn't fully acknowledge how invasive and sweeping the connections formed by cigarettes actually are. The circuit is majestic. I don't know where it begins or ends (does anyone?), but it moves from indigenous myths of tobacco gods, into the sublime symbolism of Baudelaire, across factory floors, hovers above the head of Sartre, filters through my grandfather's lungs in his ball turret during World War II, is expelled in Kerouac's ebullient breath, is crushed onto canvases, seared into cells of film, moves through the houses of my relatives and into my own lungs in Iraq before connecting to the words on this page and moving into you. Words like cigarettes burning for a moment before crumbling into ash.

Chapter 6

Tradition

I vividly remember the morning of September 11, 2001 because it felt like the world was ending. Or, rather, that at least one world was ending and we were collectively being shoved from what had been a kind of bland but comfortably predictable post-Cold War American ecosystem of nascent globalization, burgeoning internet, and managerial neoliberal politics into…what? There wasn't a name for it yet. Maybe there still isn't. Minerva's owl has yet to fly. But the maw of entropic change opened wide enough and we fell in.

I was a senior at a suburban high school in the American Middle West. In my earliest class that day, Pre-Calculus, when Flight 11 crashed into the North Tower. After the second plane hit the South Tower, an announcement was made over the intercom system and a few classrooms with access to televisions wheeled them in on carts and turned the news on. Classes went on normally, but there was a muted fear, a muffled terror that was as thrilling as it was tragic. Something momentous was happening. History was happening. And it was disgusting.

My class after Pre-Calculus was an electronic music composition elective. No televisions in the classroom, but keyboards and computers covering every available surface. That day we were composing fake commercial jingles. Simple, repetitive ear worms that would entice customers to buy things. The goal as I saw it was to use sound to create a sort of alternate world, a pocket outside of time and space, untouched by entropy. A digital choir of fake angels for a consumer paradise. I remember that other kids in the class were distracted by the news and totally unable to work, with their headphones half on and gossiping. But the day's events had the opposite effect on me, and with great care I plunked away at the keyboard searching for melodic lines which seemed delicately reconstructed from a half-decayed dream.

> Suddenly we found ourselves living in a kind of Year Zero, in which everything we knew of the world before could now be dismissed as "Pre-9/11 thinking." Never strong in our knowledge of history, North Americans had become a blank slate – "a clean sheet of paper" on which "the newest and most beautiful words can be written," as Mao said of his people. A new army of experts materialized to write new and beautiful words on the receptive canvass of our posttrauma consciousness: "clash of civilizations," they inscribed. "Axis of evil," "Islamo-fascism," "homeland security."
> Naomi Klein, *Shock Doctrine*

Of course I was making electronic shopping music on 9/11. What was George W. Bush's advice to Americans after the attacks? Keep shopping. Go to the mall. Nothing has to fundamentally change so long as we keep up the pretense of late-capitalism. The songs that I was creating in class were something akin to Muzak, the ghostly watercolor sounds of bland shopping mall consumerism. The sonic equivalent of potted ferns and food court skylights. Those tones, homeless as they were, seeming to emanate from a non-place where history didn't exist and time itself distended into an everlasting but sedate shopping spree, would follow me to Iraq. In my mind, they would become associated with the sounds of our hypnagogic empire. No trumpets. No war drums. No frothing citizenry, but a luxury automotive commercial on loop. The dead tones of easy listening. A driverless car cruising through an anonymous cityscape. And like a casino interior, no clocks or windows to an external reality.

In joining the Army and going to Iraq, I wanted some kind of escape from the nihilistic music of the consumer capitalist ghost world. I want to confront the Real, in a real place and in real history. And eventually, after the war, I would find a music that would both echo my desire as well as give me a sort of retroactive perspective on the illusion of dead eternity that I was trying to escape.

Heaven is a place / A place where nothing / Nothing ever happens
Talking Heads, Heaven

Eventually, years after I desperately and almost ironically created commercial jingles on 9/11, I would find the music appropriate to the American consumer non-time and non-place. Vaporwave – the only music genre to live and die completely on the internet – is a kind of DIY electronic music, unconsciously heavy with the ethos of punk, which appropriates the sounds of malls, 80s and 90s smooth jazz and R&B, and early internet sound ecologies. Springing up on message boards and chat rooms in the mid-naughts, vaporwave is a micro-generation's response to the failed promises of consumer capitalism. Chopped, looped and muffled Muzak that resembles a segment of a half-remembered dream, gauzy with nostalgia and unfulfilled desire. An 80s radio hit smeared into a drone which never crescendos or changes. Snippets of commercials amateurishly pasted over a dull beat. The sounds you imagine when you meditate on an undead plastic plant in an abandoned mall. Its undecayed leaves covered with a thin film of dust. Strange echoes from the abandoned shops.

In my own mind, the collapse of the World Trade Center towers on 9/11, the intentional manipulation of the soundtracks of our consumerist fantasies, and the dematerialization of linear time into a vapor are all connected. Time flattens and distends into a cool pile of rubble. The past is unavailable. The future is an empty promise. Damaged Muzak repeats on a loop forever.

In his wonderful *Babbling Corpse: Vaporwave and the Commodification of Ghosts*, Grafton Tanner writes:

With the realization of global capitalism, postmodern art pulls from various times and places to create a pastiche that reflects the commodification of culture without necessarily critiquing it openly. Rampant consumerism allows artists to willfully mix media to create a new form of artistic appropriation that erases time and space, a move that foreshadows the hauntology of the twenty-first century. These various forms of postmodern art, according to Jameson, complicate our relationship with history by turning it into a commodity.

Vaporwave sketches a caricature of that commodification, laying bare in visceral terms our diseased relationship with time. We continue to meditate on the fake fern in the abandoned mall. We're turned into ghosts stuck in a perpetual now, haunting our own desires.

> *The temple is holy because it is not for sale.*
> Ezra Pound, Cantos

The energy of vaporwave as a genre, the medium that the music traffics in, is a superannuated sort of nostalgia for a dream we felt the warmth of but could never actually hold. Nostalgia feels timeless, but is a relatively modern phenomenon. The Greek segments of the word itself literally mean "longing for home," and though we've been searching for our homecoming since long before Odysseus, the word itself is relatively new. Svetlana Boym, in *The Future of Nostalgia*, tells us that the word was created by Johannes Hofer, a Swiss doctor, in 1688, and from the very beginning it was associated with sound. Formulated first as a medical condition instead of a poetic artifact or philosophical construct, nostalgia could be triggered by any number of things but especially old songs from a lost homeland. The whistle of a half-remembered lullaby. The humming of a familiar tune. The haunted music of ghosts. Dr Albert von Haller wrote that "[o] ne of the earliest symptoms [of nostalgia] is hearing the voice of a person one loves in the voice of another with whom one is conversing..." Sound itself became a wound, or a rupture through which nostalgia can enter. Or a melancholy disguise covering the voice of the immediate. Boym writes:

> Similarly, Scots, particularly Highlanders, were known to succumb to incapacitating nostalgia when hearing the sound of the bagpipes – so much so, in fact, that their military superiors had to prohibit them from playing, singing or even whistling native tunes in a suggestive manner.
>
> Jean-Jacques Rousseau writes about the effects of cowbells, the rustic sounds that excite in the Swiss joys of life and youth and a bitter sorrow for having lost them. The music in this case "does not act precisely as music, but as a memorative sign." The music of home, whether a rustic cantilena or a pop song, is the permanent accompaniment of nostalgia – its ineffable charm that makes the nostalgic teary-eyed and tongue-tied and often clouds critical reflection on the subject.

Heard in this context, vaporwave is the musical deconstruction and reconstitution of our tongue-tied nostalgia for a consumer paradise which never quite panned out. A homeland that we miss without having ever fully inhabited.

From its beginning, nostalgia was associated with soldiers. The Swiss were mercenaries and often found themselves far-afield, pulled away from the familiar sounds of mountains, idylls and dairy farms to fight in foreign lands. When we think of people who miss their homeland, people with a great love for home who for one reason or another are forced to leave, we think of refugees, exiles and soldiers. But they've always existed. People have always been forced to leave home, sometimes permanently, for one reason or another. What makes nostalgia a modern condition?

We turn again to Boym, who writes:

Modern nostalgia is a mourning for the impossibility of mythical return, for the loss of an enchanted world with clear borders and values; it could be a secular expression of a spiritual longing, a nostalgia for an absolute, a home that is both physical and spiritual, the edenic unity of time and space before entry into history. The nostalgic is looking for a spiritual addressee. Encountering silence, he looks for memorable signs, desperately misreading them.

And as a soldier who's suffered the pangs of nostalgia, how could I disagree? To take Boym's analysis a step further, however, I'd be willing to bet that the same Highlanders who broke down at the sound of bagpipes suffered from nostalgia long before they set foot in a foreign land. Nostalgia, a longing for temporal and spatial continuity, a desire for a settled home in the world, was probably the reason why they left home in the first place. I think of my time before the Army, sitting in the lurid glare of my familiar suburban diner longing for a more absolute familiarity with the universe. The past and present facing each other as two mirrors creating the illusion of an infinite regression.

Boym again writes that:

The diagnosis of the disease of nostalgia in the late seventeenth century took place roughly at the historical moment when the conception of time and history were undergoing radical change. The religious wars in Europe came to an end but the much prophesied end of the world and doomsday did not occur...It is customary to perceive "linear" Judeo-Christian time in opposition to the "cyclical" pagan time of eternal return and discuss both with the help of spatial metaphors. What this opposition obscures is the temporal and historical development of the perception of time that since [the]

Renaissance on has become more and more secularized, severed from cosmological vision.

Dreams of progress and nostalgic reveries are both manifestations of this non-time, this in-between conception of time. Time itself has become nonhuman, measured by isotopic decay, bytes and market fluctuations. And so we cry when we hear bagpipes and church bells. We rightfully feel robbed and bereft.

I joined the Army because I wanted temporal coherence. I wanted access to the past and the future instead of being isolated at the center of an infinite refraction, stuck halfway between a past I couldn't touch and a future which never came. Like a life without hierarchy, a life without a sense of vertical time – of feeling an existential connection to both the past and the future – is just another form of isolation. The mall is abandoned. The fern is dead. The strange noises you hear coming from the empty shops are just the echoes of your own movements.

And as I sat there brooding on the old, unknown world, I thought of Gatsby's wonder when he first picked out the green light at the end of Daisy's dock. He had come a long way to this blue lawn, and his dream must have seemed so close that he could hardly fail to grasp it. He did not know that it was already behind him, somewhere back in that vast obscurity beyond the city, where the dark fields of the republic rolled on under the night.

Gatsby believed in the green light, the orgastic future that year by year recedes before us. It eluded us then, but that's no matter — to-morrow we will run faster, stretch out our arms farther.

And one fine morning — —

So we beat on, boats against the current, borne back ceaselessly into the past.

F Scott Fitzgerald, *The Great Gatsby*

The name of the unit I served in occasionally changed as the leadership higher up jostled around and the chain of command consistently reorganized, but the core group of men I served with remained relatively stable. Even as we moved from Germany to Iraq and back again, the sense of stability remained. It wasn't a geographic stability, anchored to a specific place, but we were instead held together by a temporal bond. We were held together in, by and through time.

It happened on at least three different levels. We were held together through time in three ways. The first was the personal. Some of the guys I served with I had known all the way from basic training in the pines of Ft Benning. And we were held together by our shared memories, which were strengthened as we continued to accumulate more of them through the war. The memories themselves took on different tones depending on what they referred to. There were minor chord progressions of our shared hardships, like our frozen to the bone field exercises in Germany before deployment or the rough first few weeks at a remote combat outpost. There were the bold major chord lifts of adventures. Road trips to Prague. Triumphant raids where no one made a mistake and everyone felt courageous and competent. The doors collapsed, weapons caches were discovered and everyone made it back to the combat outpost in time for morning chow. But my favorite by far were the memories of jokes that we carried with us across countries and continents. The practical jokes, like hiding meatballs in each other's rucksacks or plastic utensils in ammo pouches. The strange origins of nicknames. Or the dark, surreal humor that didn't necessarily refer to anything specific but was instead a kind of stratum accumulated from the ambient violence, fear and boredom. Obscene impressions of fictional characters. Free flow gibberish and uncanny noises. As baffling as it might be, even that sort of humor provided the coordinates to a time and place that we shared together. And in the end, it didn't matter if we were complaining about past deprivation, bragging about a mission gone well, or laughing hysterically at a nonsensical sound. What mattered is that we had all been there together. What mattered was our shared past.

If we had our shared personal history, we also had our shared unit history. When I joined the Army my permanent duty station – where I would live when I wasn't deployed – was Germany, and for a long time (although it's not the case any longer), the First Infantry Division was a major American infantry unit in Europe. It was called The Big Red One after its simple insignia, a red numeral one on a green background. And having served in The Big Red One, it also became a part of my identity. This might be difficult for a secular civilian to understand, how one could feel connected to individuals they've never met through membership of an organization that exists through multiple life spans. The further out you move from identification with your own day to day experiences, the more your expression of a collective identity resists articulation and takes on reverential, almost mystical tones. Suffice to say that we sang *The Big Red One Song*, written in 1943 by then Captain Donald Kellet as he convalesced in Algeria, while we marched along German streets that the unit had helped to liberate. We felt the past inside of us. Our past. And we knew it was ours not only because we wore the same colors and carried the same guidon as the ones who had come before us, but because we remembered them and their sacrifices as we understood that ours would be remembered by subsequent generations.

As difficult as it might be for civilians to understand the weighty sense of belonging to a specific military unit, it's probably even harder to understand the third way that as infantrymen we were held together through time. In some ways, though, it's the most fundamental. Wars change as technology changes. Political regimes rise and fall. Society fluctuates in a continuous scramble toward goals that themselves shift with time. But anyone who has been a grunt working the front lines of whatever war was happening will have felt, even fleetingly, the enigmatic connection to any other, for lack of a better term, warrior. Not only is this connection widely perceived in war, but like the other two levels of temporal confederation, it's even nourished. It's possible that people who join up are temperamentally predisposed to want this kind of connection, but what sort of connection is it, exactly? It isn't quite nostalgia, a naive craving for a return to the past. And it isn't quite nostalgia's inverse, a longing for progress toward some distant future. It's more like a synthesis of past and future that would serve as an alternative to both nostalgia and progress. The proper term for it might be the maintenance of tradition.

Yves Congar, the Dominican theologian whose thoughts about tradition played such a significant role during the Second Vatican Council, defines it as coming from:

> the Latin traditio, the noun of the verb tradere, "to transmit," "to deliver." It was a term of ratification in Roman law: for example, the legal transfer of a shop or house was accompanied by the act of handing over its keys, traditio clavium; the sale of a piece of land was accompanied by the act of handing over a clod of earth. Tradere, traditio meant "to hand over an object," with the intention, on the one hand, of parting with it, and, on the other, of acquiring it. Tradere implied giving over and surrendering something to someone, passing an object from the possession of the donor to the receiver. In Greek, paradidonai, aorist paradounai, had the same meaning. An equally good simile would be that of a relay race, where the runners, spaced at intervals, pass an object from one to the other, a baton, for example, or a torch.

Congar's theological aim was to balance the claims of the written Gospel against the unwritten traditions of the Catholic church, but his work floods a light into the rich interiority of the concept of tradition more generally, as well. If history is one thing, preserved in text and referred to with something resembling a legalistic attention, then tradition, in its fullest sense, is a sort of living out the demands of the past for the sake of the future.

Tradition has an almost ambivalent relationship with text. Congar compares the difference between text and tradition to instruction versus upbringing. One is tightly focused, narrow in perspective and almost overwrought with intentionality. Tradition on the other hand is diffuse, more pervasive and works with a nearly unconscious energy. Congar writes that:

> Education does not consist in receiving a lesson from afar, which may be learned by heart and recited, thanks to a good memory, but in the daily contact and inviting example of adult life, which is mature, confident and sure of its foundations; which asserts itself simply by being what it is, and presents itself as an ideal: which someone still unsure and unformed, in search of fulfillment and in need of security, will progressively come to resemble, almost unconsciously and without effort. A child receives the life of the community into which he enters, together with the cultural riches of the preceding generations (tradition!), which are inculcated by the actions and habits of everyday life.

And then a few paragraphs later, "Tradition, like education, is a living communication whose content is inseparable from the act by which one living person hands it on to another. A written text, on the other hand, exists in its own right."

But tradition also suggests variation through repetition as much as it implies continuity through transmission. The Homeric epics were first transcribed during a fascinating historical inflection point between the passing of the Dark Ages and the emergence of Classical Antiquity. Before being transcribed, the epics had been performed for generations by itinerant bards, most likely illiterate, who kept the epics alive inside of themselves, literally in their bodies. On their breath. In their minds.

It wasn't until fairly recently that we came to understand how exactly this oral tradition was transmitted. American linguist Milman Parry studied the performance of rural epic singers in Yugoslavia in the 1930s but died before his student Albert Lord could complete and publish his study as *The Singer of Tales*. Lord writes in the book that "An oral poem is not composed for but in performance." Each performance of the epic was unique, reflecting not only the idiosyncratic style of the performer, but transforming to meet the demands of the audience. The characters didn't alter much, and the story lines remained relatively stable, but the tradition of the epic itself was preserved and transmitted through a sort of variation in repetition.

It's easier for us in our time to understand the variation rather than the repetition. Self-expression needs no defense in our world. But the repetition implies adherence to something outside of ourselves. The oral poets made their story travel, but always within the coordinates of some known and cherished land. The repetition implies ritual.

In *The Dominion of the Dead*, Robert Pogue Harrison writes about the Euro-Mediterranean mourning rituals observed by Ernesto De Martino in *Morte e pianto ritual*, noting that:

> ...the ritual lament consists in rehearsed and highly formalized gestures of externalization whose purpose is first and foremost to depersonalize the condition of grief by submitting it to a set of public, traditionally transmitted codes. By dictating the rules for "how one mourns," ritual lament helps assure that the psychic crisis engendered by loss, especially in its early stages, will not plunge the mourner into sheer delirium or catalepsy – or into what De Martino calls "irrelative" manifestations of grief. Ritualization thus serves to contain

the crises of grief in the very act of objectifying its contents through scripted gestures and precise codes of enactment.

A tradition of applying ritualistic guides to individual experience gives the articulation of those experiences form and meaning. The bards of the oral epics weren't babbling incoherently in front of crowds of bored strangers. They were operating within a tradition in order to fully commune with their audience.

There's a transformative element to the repetition of tradition. One thing can become another. Dead matter can be resurrected. Unbearable grief can be transposed into something emotionally choate. The entropic decay of the world can be interrupted, moment by moment. Conversely, without these repetitions and completely denuded of tradition, things can become almost de-sanctified. Subjects decay into objects. Simone Weil writes about The Iliad that "[t]o define force – it is that x that turns anybody who is subjected to it into a thing. Exercised to its limit, it turns a man into a thing in the most literal sense; it makes a corpse out of him." She points to the dead chariot drivers, which are dragged through the dust, bereft of any ceremonial burial, and how they're called "dearer to the vultures" than to their own wives. Giambattista Vico writes in *The New Science* that the three institutions of humanhood are burial, matrimony and religion. Bereft of their gods, unburied and with vultures instead of wives, the dead chariot drivers have become inhuman.

To be human is to bury our dead. Vico writes that the Latin *humanitas* comes from *humando*, to bury. We fully come into ourselves as humans through the tradition of connecting ourselves visceral with the past. Commenting on this, Robert Pogue Harrison writes that "As human beings we are born of the dead – of the regional ground they occupy, of the languages they inhabited, of the worlds they brought into being, of the many institutional, legal, cultural and psychological legacies that, through us, connect them to the unborn." Without acknowledging this rich and enigmatic link with the past, we objectify ourselves. Without ceremony, tradition becomes history, human potentialities are flattened to a horizontal plane, and our deepest modes of connection die individually with each person if they're ever discovered at all.

The most fundamental symbol of tradition, of human interaction across time, is the grave. As Lewis Mumford writes in *The City in History*, "Mid the uneasy wanderings of paleolithic man, the dead were the first to have a permanent dwelling: a cavern, a mound marked by a cairn, a collective barrow. These were landmarks to which the living probably returned at intervals, to commune with or placate the ancestral spirits." In the economics of human legacy, as we fulfill our duty to the dead by marking signs of their existence, we simultaneously fulfill an obligation to ourselves and the generations to follow us. The original purpose of a home, before the living occupied permanent structures, was the housing of the dead. As Robert Pogue Harrison explains, "To inhabit the world humanly one must be a creature of legacy. That explains why the living housed the dead before they housed themselves. They placed them in graves, coffins, urns – in any case they placed them in something that we call their resting place so that their legacies could be retrieved and their afterlives perpetuated." In this sense both graves and houses are reflected in each other's images, bound together in the shared purpose of sustaining humans in their humanity through the vagaries of time. But the symbolic energy of graves and houses spills over the boundaries of the literal objects themselves. We bury our dead in songs. We inhabit cultural legacy. And the purpose of both changes relatively little. Harrison continues:

> The "in" that the dead abide in – whether it be in the earth, in our memory, in our institutions, in our genes, in our words, in our books, in our dreams, in our hearts, in our

prayers or in our thoughts – this "in" of the dead defines the human interiority which our houses build walls around and render inhabitable. The domestic interior is thus in some fundamental sense mortuary, inhabited not only by the dead but also by the unborn in their projective potentiality. It is because we are the ligature between the dead and the unborn – and not because we are vulnerable to the elements and predators – that we humans require housing. All of which corroborates the following proposition: A house is a place of insideness in the openness of nature where the dead, through the care of the living, perpetuate their afterlives and promote the interests of the unborn.

Perhaps the most horrifying expression of the disruption of the bond between the living and the dead, between the home and the grave, is the 1982 Tobe Hooper film *Poltergeist*. In the film, a typical suburban California family called the Freelings begins to experience a haunting that quickly goes from exciting and playful to terrifying. Eventually the youngest daughter is sort of "kidnapped" and taken to a spiritual realm by a quasi-demonic entity. The parents, with the assistance of a medium, are eventually able to recover their daughter from the metaphysical plane.

That's a skeletal outline of the plot, but what the movie is actually about is something less occult and far more fundamental, far more human in the Vichean sense. The father of the family, played by Craig T Nelson, is a sales representative for the property development company which owns his sprawling neighborhood, Cuesta Verde. During a revealing moment of the film, Mr Freeling's boss takes him to a hill above the metastasizing neighborhood to offer a vision of future growth. In the valley below them are the sprawling, anonymous, identical suburban homes and cul de sacs. On the hill above them is a graveyard that would need to be "relocated" in order for the growth to take place. "That's sacrilegious, isn't it?", asks Mr Freeling. To which his boss replies, "Don't worry about it. After all, it's not ancient tribal burial grounds. It's just people. Besides, we've done it before..." Revealing that a cemetery was displaced in order to build the home that the Freelings currently live in. Later, in the climax of the film, Mr Freeling screams at his boss, "You son of a bitch! You moved the cemetery, but you left the bodies, didn't you? You son of a bitch, you left the bodies and you only moved the headstones!"

The philosopher Zizek tells us in *A Pervert's Guide To Cinema* that if you really want to understand what's going on in a horror movie, simply remove the supernatural element. In *Poltergeist*, it's obvious that what's going on is that the relationship between the living and the dead has been betrayed by the living. In the name of economic growth. In the name of progress. In the name of striving toward a cheap and careless ease of living that's revealed in the very name of the family being haunted, the Freelings, a kind of portmanteau of "feeling" and "free." It's a particularly American dream, achieving complete and total "liberation" from the past; but as Mr Freeling's boss intimates, the past is just "people," and when we betray our traditional duties to the people of the past it's the generations which follow us that suffer the worse for it.

Contained in the opposition between Cuesta Verde, the suburban neighborhood of new and identical but soulless houses, and its mirrored opposite cemetery on the hill composed of rows of soulful but moldering abodes for the dead, is a synecdoche for American amnesia of the past. America is a land of forgetting. It's a country haunted by half-removed burial grounds and abandoned buildings. The names of places sink into the Earth and are forgotten. George Stewart writes in *Names on the Land* that, "Why so many names vanished is not hard to explain. A name could live only in continuing tradition, and a mere notation upon a map or a journal – no matter how high-sounding – was only a hope of the man who wrote it." Anyone growing up in suburban America like I did has felt the claustrophobic grip of that permanent present, of every name and concept existing as notations upon a map without a living tradition to sustain them. Writing of memory and World War I in *The Missing of the Somme*, Geoff Dyer makes the claim that "The issue, in short, is not simply the way the war generates memory but the way that memory has determined – and continues to determine – the meaning of war." His argument, and it isn't exactly wrong, is that the war was sort of remembered in reverse, with the battles and gore struggling to live up to a pre-anticipated sense of nostalgia for sacrifice. He makes a compelling case. But what Dyer might leave underrepresented is how this sense of nostalgia is an overreaction more generally to the death of tradition. What the great moments to the fallen of the Somme actually anticipate is the death of tradition itself. They're warnings of what happens when we move the headstones and construct an amnesiac progress over the bones of the dead. Not on a personal level, but as a culture. The fears of the great monument builders weren't unfounded. After 16 years of the Global War on Terror, a national memorial is still cutting through red tape in order to be constructed. What held it up is that according to an obscure law, a war must have been over for 10 years before a memorial is constructed to honor its fallen. But the Global War on Terror, by its very nature, continues endlessly. This is the very definition of cultural amnesia, of the living forgetting the dead and the young paying the price.

Jane and Louise Wilson have photographed in black and white the massive, abstract fortifications along the French Atlantic coastline. Moldering hulks that were once a part of Hitler's Atlantic Wall defense, they resemble concrete machines discarded by time travelers. Or the remnants of an advanced ancient civilization. The casual beach walker coming from another hemisphere might be shocked and confused to come across them. Their presence, simultaneously expressing both the decay of time and the persistence of corporeality, is more disturbing the less we know about their origins. They're Ozymandias' "vast and trunkless legs of stone" without the explicit pathos of an ironic inscription. We see them and we're haunted by an unarticulated past. In an inverse of *Poltergeist*, we're left with abstract tombstones gesturing at absent bodies. And we're stricken by guilt that we've made the dead strangers. That we've forgotten the ones who came before us. Robert Harrison writes that:

> We are all latecomers. To be human means to come after those who came before. Just as we are always preceded by our forebears, so too the ground in which we lay them to rest has always been ready to receive the bones of others – "others" in the most radical sense of the term, including that of other species, many of whom have died on our behalf.

Because it deals in death, war can be a respite from forgetting. In it a nexus is formed connecting the current living to each other, their fellow soldiers, the history of their unit and army, and even deeper into a quasi-mystical web of cultural associations and characters. Most current war writing emphasizes the personal experience and how the combat might fit into today's political contexts. War epics of the nineteenth century emphasized something similar. Vast casts of individuals moved through a larger drama that they themselves could never hope to apprehend, but which was still fundamentally diurnal in its scope. Writing from within a Modernist, experimental and in some senses more pre-modern mode, David Jones bypasses the banal individual existentialism of the contemporary war novel and instead illuminates the way that organized combat connects participants through time. What he says about the war and the past in his preface to *In Parenthesis* is worth quoting at length:

I suppose at no time did one so much live with a consciousness of the past, the very remote, and the more immediate and trivial past, both superficially and more subtly. No one, I suppose, however much not given to association, could see infantry in tin-hats, with ground-sheets over their shoulders, with sharpened pine-stakes in the hands, and not recall

"...or may we carm,
Within this wooden O..."

But there were deeper complexities of sight and sound to make ever present

"the pibble pabble in Pompey's camp"

Every man's speech and habit of mind were a perpetual showing: now of Napier's expedition, now of the Legions at the Wall, now of "train-band captain," now of Jack Cade, of John Ball, of the commons in arms. Now of High Germany, of Dolly Gray, of Bullcalf, Wartand Poins; of Jingo largenesses, of things as small as the kingdom of Elmet; of Wellington's raw shire recruits, of ancient border antipathies, of our contemporary, less intimate, larger unities, of John Barleycorn, of "sweet Sally Frampton." Now of Coel Hên – of the Celtic cycle that lies, a subterranean influence as a deep water troubling, under every trump in this Island, like Merlin complaining under his big rock.

Not all moments in a war adhere easily with the past. In my own experiences, filling radios or fixing electronics, using computers and phone banks to call loved ones, were moments outside of the war. But there were times when the air between the past and the future thinned, and it felt like being high in the seat of memory. Standing guard. Taking prisoners. Disposing of the dead. Seeking cover. Sleeping next to your comrades. Being dirty and hungry and far away from home. Joking through the suffering. Or bragging through it. Perhaps the most powerful scene in Jones' In Parenthesis is when the old soldier Dai

Greatcoat weaves typical soldierly boasting into a tapestry of historical and mythical bravery and suffering. His brag becomes the ur-brag of all soldiers for all time, moving as it does between continents and epochs. It's the grandest brag a soldier has ever been made to utter, and it's all the more true because of that:

My fathers were with the Black Prinse of Wales
at the passion of
the blind Bohemian king.
They served in these fields,
it is in the histories that you can read it, Corporal – boys
Gower, they were – it is writ down- yes.
Wot about Methuselum, Taffy?
I was with Abel when his brother found him,
under the green tree.
I built a shit-house for Artaxerxes.
I was the spear in Balin's hand
that made waste King Pellam's land.

The song goes on for pages. And it does achieve a grandeur that deserves to be called a song. If vaporwave, the empty and sad soundtrack to a permanent now, was the music of my return to the civilian world, then Dai Greatcoat's boast was the song of the military. Robert Harrison explains the differences between the two modes of music when he writes that "Where the dead are simply dead, the living are in some sense already dead as well. Conversely, where the afterlife of the dead receives new life, the Earth as a whole receives a new blessing." Vaporwave was the music of falsity – of an equally artificial sense of both progress and nostalgia. An anti-tradition. Dai Greatcoat's song is the boast of tradition, through which the breath of life passes freely among the living, the dead and the future.

Chapter 7

Honor

Zorba: Why do the young die? Why does anybody die?
Basil: I don't know.
Zorba: What's the use of all your damn books? If they don't
tell you that, what the hell do they tell you?
Basil: They tell me about the agony of men who can't answer
questions like yours.
Zorba: I spit on their agony.
Michael Cacoyannis, *Zorba the Greek*

I don't believe I used the word "honor" much before joining the
Army. I'm certain I didn't use it very often after I separated.
Even more than hierarchy, ceremony or community, it's honor
that defines the shape of the military experience. It's honor that
gives military service coherence. And it's honor which all the
other attributes of the Army depend on for meaning, like the
syntax of a language. In *Henry IV*, Shakespeare has Falstaff say
that honor is just "A word," a "scutcheon," or gravestone, meant
to spur men on to pointless deaths. But as Prince Hal reminds
the miscreant knight, everyone owes God a death. And it's the
sense of honor, much more than an empty word, which imbues
our ending with meaningful significance. It's honor which keeps
us from suffering the fate of Nietzsche's last man, scurrying for
comfort and security but without being quite sure why. Honor
keeps us from confusing means with ends.

In many ways, honor resists precise definition. The official
United States Army website says of honor:

Of all the Army values, honor is the one that embodies all the
others. Honor is a matter of carrying out, acting, and living

112

the values of respect, duty, loyalty, selfless service, integrity and personal courage in everything you do, according to the Army. We feel honor while listening to our National Anthem or watching the posting of the colors. We show honor by recognizing the outstanding contributions made by other Soldiers and civilians. We give honor to the flag and to the ideals it represents and the symbolism it lends to the greatness of our nation.

So honor is an action and a feeling both. It's a unique sort of energy which can only be ascertained by its effects, like electrons moving through a wire. The Army claims that honor "embodies" each of the other "Army values." It's what animates them and allows them to take form. That being so, "honor" becomes more significant than the sum of its parts, with more coherence than a jumbled amalgamation of otherwise unrelated values. It means more than simply following the rules. Honor, in the sense that I experienced it in the military, more closely resembles an ongoing decision, an act of will or perhaps faith, that following the rules has significance beyond professional self-preservation.

The Prussian military theorist Carl von Clausewitz is usually associated with the phrase "the fog of war," a pithy expression describing what he regarded as the most fundamental aspect of combat: confusion. Confusion about your own abilities and resources. Confusion about geography. Confusion about the intention and abilities of your enemy. In *On War* he wrote that: "War is the realm of uncertainty; three-quarters of the factors on which action in war is based are wrapped in a fog of greater or lesser uncertainty. A sensitive and discriminating judgment is called for; a skilled intelligence to scent out the truth." Clausewitz was of course writing for the benefit of his fellow Prussian officers who would lead soldiers in combat. But the same confusion exists for the Sergeant or Private on the battlefield as well, and perhaps then with an even more intimidating purity.

The fog of war that settles on the battlefield can be a literal fog, a blanketing by the elements which mutes or distorts the senses. You might not be able to tell where sounds are emanating from. Dust covers friendly positions. And in Iraq, enemy and non-enemy blend into one another, occasionally changing roles and taking places.

But there's also a figurative fog that covers everything, which can accurately be described as a moral chaos. I imagine this chaos has more psychological (as well as physical) room to expand in a nonconventional war, where the moral calculus is complicated by the battlefield being temporarily and yet almost perpetually placed in the middle of a civilian area – now that the line between wartime and peacetime, between the front and the rear, has evaporated. It doesn't help that we've also convinced ourselves to rely so heavily on rational and technical controls, things such as official Rules of Engagement, high-end optics and Blue Force Trackers to tell friend and foe apart. The military world is just as inundated with a technocratic mindset as the civilian world, if not more so. But guidelines fail. Technology fails. The rules fail. And so honor is there, a bright seam of energy running through the opacity of combat which we can rely on almost like a moral failsafe.

There's a contradiction, though, at the heart of how honor works. It's a fixed point, a final bedrock set of assumptions about behavior and responsibilities. But there isn't one single set of rules of honor. Cultures which we consider "honor cultures" – and the list is a long one – each have their own honor values, many of which contradict each other. And of course honor systems change with time. They adapt. Honor is both a hard ideal which guides through chaos and a shifting set of rules which adapt themselves to evolving circumstances. An interesting point of comparison might be the Chinese notion of *quan*, or law. The philosopher Byung-Chul Han writes in his book *Shanzhai: Deconstruction in Chinese* that *quan*:

...contains a semantic range that gives the Chinese notion of law or rights a special cast. In particular it lacks any notion of finality, absoluteness or invariability. Literally *quan* means the weight that can be slid back and forth on a sliding-weight scale. Thus in the first place *quan* means to weigh or assess. It has no fixed, final position. Rather, it is moveable, adjustable and provisional, like the sliding weight on the scale. It changes its position according to the weight of its counterpart in order to achieve balance. As a law it is balancing, not excluding or ostracizing. Exclusiveness is alien to it. Of course, Chinese thought is also familiar with the regularities of conventional norms (*jing*), but at the same time it is strongly influenced by the awareness of continuous change. In Zhu Xi we find the following saying…"Under normal conditions we adhere to the rules of convention, but in times of change we use *quan*."

Honor as I've understood and experienced it is the *quan* of combat when the rules have deteriorated, and the predictable conventions have broken down.

What does the sliding weight of honor help us to achieve? What are we measuring? What does its malleable precision allow us to participate in? Unfortunately, honor has the reputation of only being considered itself in the most extreme examples. Someone drinking at a bar is insulted and feels the need to fight their antagonist. A family feud, senseless to outsiders, lasts for generations. A person who's been socially shamed kills themselves. Honor is at work in each of these instances, of course, but it's honor at its most lurid – and its most alien to contemporary Western (particularly cosmopolitan) sensibilities. But honor works peacefully and piecemeal, too.

Tamler Sommers writes in *Why Honor Matters* that "Hospitality remains of central importance in honor cultures today. If you've traveled widely, chances are you've received the warmest welcomes in countries characterized as honor cultures, and it can be a shock returning home to a society without the same commitment to hospitality." The guest-host relationship of what we call honor cultures, cultures unswayed by the legalistic universalism of the Enlightenment, has a dignity, grandeur and sweetness that's difficult for us to understand. We want things to have an almost self-referential utility. We want conflict to be resolved by an "objective" third party. But the swaying weight of honor belies a much deeper commitment to value as value than our tepid ad hoc atomistic morality allows us to understand. Even so, we engage in simple forms of honor here and there in our own culture. Some schools use honor codes. We try to honor our bodies with exercise. We honor our friendships and loved ones with selfless loyalty. The definition of honor might be a moving target, sometimes ending in violence, other times resulting in humble acts of hospitality, but what seems to be the overarching commonality of honor in its various forms, the root at the genus of honor, is an existential commitment to value itself.

Because honor is so slippery, shifting and changing from culture to culture and time to place, its external characteristics are mutable. Better to look at its mechanics, at how the thing itself operates in any given situation. At what it does and how it works. The most obvious function, as I said, is to reach beyond utilitarianism and toward a larger, more comprehensive reality. This is why honor is often bound up with the mythopoetic. Honor practices, to borrow a phrase from Eric Voegelin in the context of the function of novels, "relate existent things to a ground that will endow their existence with meaning." This kind of transcendence is less a stable objective thing and more of an experience. A state of being in the world while attuning yourself to the larger ineffable reality just beyond your grasp. What might appear as irrationality is a commitment to orienting yourself toward a field of reality which makes "value" itself plausible.

Maybe the phrase "transcendent reality" is misleading. Maybe "extended reality" is more appropriate. Honor allows for dynamism on a grand scale, creating a space for things as gargantuan and oppositional as banishment and redemption. Honor opens us up to the possibility of radical and fundamental internal change, which our day to day laws and regulations tactfully eschew. There's of course an anodyne wisdom to legalism sans honor. That wisdom is so obvious to us as to be conventional and hardly needs defending here. Next to it, honor might appear amoral to our modern eyes. James Bowman writes in *Honor: A History* that:

> Morality is nuanced and subtle; there are shades of right and wrong, innocence and guilt. Honor is stark and unforgiving: either you fight or you run; either you are a hero or a coward; either you are chaste or a whore. Everything about it is at odds with the spirit of our age: so analytical, so psychological, so non-"judgmental" and so much in love with nuance, irony, and ambiguity.

Bowman is partially correct. Honor does stand at odds with the spirit of our age. But honor also has its own sense of nuance and ambiguity. The difference is that honor's nuance expresses itself over a longer stretch of time. Where as contemporary morality mines context out of mitigating circumstances, honor allows itself to unfold slowly through the lifespan of, not just an individual person, but an entire people. Contemporary moral nuance is about accumulation: of facts, data, plot points. The dynamics of honor move across the spectrum of narrative and are so grounded in the fundament of action that even if honor is less capricious about change and nuance as contemporary legalism might be, its turns are more profound, striking almost abyssal shifts in the depths of our identity. A legalistic morality demands facts. Honor demands devotion. And time. Honor is experiential.

While in the Army I dishonored myself. It's a complicated event to touch on, and its proper treatment would demand a book all of its own, but it illustrates what I mean by honor allowing for redemption. About halfway through my first deployment to Iraq I let myself be convinced that writing about my experiences for *The New Republic* would be a good idea. My motives weren't all that terrible. It was 2006, and the war was just beginning to be seen as a lost cause by many Americans. Thinking that too many people back home were using the word "war" without quite understanding all that it entailed – the squalor, the casual cruelty, the gallows humor, the decay of communities and the wounds of the combatants – I agreed to write a few dispatches under a pseudonym. Interestingly, perhaps predictably, it was the piece focused on the gallows humor of American soldiers that caught people's attention. It wasn't long before I was found out and punished by the military.

At the time I was indignant with righteousness. What had I done but given the American public, the people in a democracy who are ultimately responsible for the wars waged in their name, true stories about the war they allowed? Most of my fellow soldiers saw it differently. They felt betrayed. War has a bivalence. Of course it's a public, political event. But it's also, by those who wage it or are touched by it, a profoundly personal occurrence so deeply entwined with identity that gossiping anecdotally to strangers about it feels like a betrayal of those very experiences. They can't simply be reduced to essaysitic form, especially as they're still in the process of being waged. Of course, some part of me understood that, and the twinge of guilt only turned my righteousness into a stronger alloy.

Most likely to an outsider, my punishment was not commensurate with my infractions. I was put on a work detail where I was made to work 20 hours a day (4 hours of sleep being the absolute minimum the Army is required to give a soldier). During the long work days I would fill sandbags and move scrap from one end of our combat outpost to another. A noncommissioned officer accompanied me wherever I was, so that I could never have a moment alone and to enforce the strict "no talking to Beauchamp" rule that my platoon sergeant had implemented. And as the ultimate symbol of dishonor, my rifle was taken from me. It was, by no stretch of the imagination, the most difficult experience I faced during the war. And it came at the hands of my fellow soldiers, my brothers. The worst of it ended when I finally contracted typhoid from a combination of exhaustion and inhaling so much Iraqi dust. Slipping in and out of consciousness while lying in a field hospital with a temperature of 103F, my body flirted with permanent brain damage. Bullets had whistled by my head. Bombs had exploded around me. But this felt as near to death as I'd ever been.

Recovering and returning to my unit was a kind of rebirth. Slowly, but definitely, I was afforded the same respect that I had had before. Maybe even more. I was shriven, had proven myself worthy to the punishment, and had achieved some kind of redemption of honor among my fellows. By the time my second deployment rolled around, I had regained my rank, become a team leader and even served for a while as the company armorer – a position of responsibility far above my rank.

I regret writing about war during war. Not because I was wrong about Americans needing to understand the ground-level reality of what they endorsed, but because it was a betrayal in the eyes of my comrades. I should have waited until after the war or after I was out of the Army. But I'm proud that I was able to pick myself back up and regain my honor. I'm grateful that such a process exists whereby I was able to be shriven and redeemed.

Honor is transpersonal and pre-political, which is why it's so difficult to define in contemporary psychological terms. To say one "has" honor is to speak analogically. As Frank Henderson

Stewart explains in *Honor*:

> ...the possession of honor is not like the possession of a true personal quality. We may say, for instance, that Jane was clever before she fell on her head, and was stupid afterwards, or that Samson lost his strength when his hair was cut. In cases of this kind we believe that some change of disposition has occurred in the individual. But a man may lose his honor without any such change: the fact that he has (say) tamely submitted to being insulted does not necessarily make him a different person. To have honor seems, then, to be like being American (in the sense of possessing US citizenship) or being poor – a quality relating to the external circumstances of the individual, which while it may change him when acquired or shed, does not necessarily do so. Like poverty, it may be closely related to certain true personal qualities without itself being one.

And so, though the particular manifestations of honor change through cultures and across time, there's a common "economy" of honor connecting them all. Honor isn't static. It's a dramatic and potentially reversible change orbiting a fixed identity.

Honor requires time. Of course, in a single moment it can be gained or reversed, but these moments, more than accumulating, cohere into a narrative. This is why honor is so closely associated with the epic. And that this narrative coherence, this unfolding through time, is lacking in our contemporary lives makes honor even more difficult for us to comprehend. Byung-Chul Han writes in *The Scent of Time* that "The decay of time goes hand in hand with the rise of mass society and increasing uniformity." What he means by the "decay of time" is the vivisection of our lives into an infinity of present moments. The sensation of life accelerating beyond our control, represented by the technology we use and the political systems which use us, denudes our lives of phenomena which require development through time. As Han writes:

> This temporal condensation also distinguishes knowledge from information, which is empty of time, so to speak – timeless in the sense of being deprived of time. Because of this temporal neutrality, information can be stored and arbitrarily retrieved. If things are deprived of memory, they become information or commodities. They are pushed into a time-free, ahistorical space. The storage of information is preceded by the deletion of memory.

Han is mostly concerned with the effect this "temporal condensation" has on contemplation and dying a good death, but honor requires a similar temporal richness in which to become its full self. It isn't simply that our values resist a full reception of honor, it's that we literally don't have time for it.

We don't normally associate honor with time or duration. We usually associate it with irrational violence. To someone standing outside of an honor tradition, this is the most obvious effect of honor. But violence occurs without honor. Certain kinds of rationality – it isn't necessary to cite the countless historical examples – not only lead to violence, but execute that violence in a much more broad, insidious and efficient manner. And honor itself isn't necessarily amoral. Honor can foster a sense of pride or be a bulwark against pathetic self-exoneration. In *The Unbearable Lightness of Being*, Milan Kundera has the novel's protagonist, Tomas, feel a deep disgust toward his fellow Czechs who complacently accepted Soviet rule. He writes that:

> When Tomas heard Communists shouting in defense of their inner purity, he said to himself, "as a result of your 'not knowing,' this country has lost its freedom, lost it for centuries, perhaps, and you shout that you feel no guilt? How

can you stand the sight of what you've done? How is it that you aren't horrified? Have you no eyes to see? If you had eyes, you would have to put them out and wander away from Thebes."

Sommers comments on the passage that, "It may be true that [the Czech collaborators] were unaware of the extent of the atrocities, but, according to Tomas, this is no excuse. They should feel deep shame for what they did to their own country. Tomas doesn't see Oedipus's perspective as irrational or pathological. He sees it as morally superior to that of his countrymen."

Seen in this light, honor has less to do with irrationality and more with the deepest sort of fidelity, or attunement, to a higher and anti-utilitarian moral purpose. Much of our modern lives are predicated upon denying this sort of attunement. If meaning requires time in order to develop, and if honor is in large part an orientation toward meaning, then our atomized sense of time struggles against our understanding of and participation with honor. Han writes that:

The cause of the shrinking present, or the disappearing of duration, is not acceleration, as many mistakenly believe. The relationship between the loss of a duration and acceleration is far more complex than that. Time tumbles on, like an avalanche, precisely because it no longer contains anything to hold on to within itself. The tearing away of time, the directionless acceleration of processes (which because of the lack of direction, is no longer really an acceleration at all), is triggered by those point-like presences between which there is no longer any temporal attraction. Acceleration in the proper sense of the word presupposes a course which directs the flow.

And so our collective sense of a loss of honor and a temporal spinning out of control are both symptoms of the same malady: the general abdication of an attunement of our lives toward collective goals and values.

Honor necessitates orientation and time, but it's more than those requirements. It also demands action. When Plato writes about the tripartite soul – the three elements of the psyche which require balance in order for a person to be just – it's *thumos*, often translated as "high-spiritedness," which we most associate with honor. *Thumos* of course must be balanced against *logos* (reason) and *epithymia* (appetite), but its presence is necessary in order to be fully human. In the most basic terms, *thumos* is the energy required to do what you need to do. Peter Sloterdijk elaborates on this theme in his book *Rage and Time*:

> In book four of the Republic, Plato presents an outline theory of *thymos* [alternate spelling of *thumos*] of great psychological richness and extensive political importance. The impressive achievement of Plato's interpretation of *thymos* consists in a person's ability to be infuriated. This turn against oneself can come about when a person does not live up to the expectations that would have to be satisfied in order for a person not to lose self-respect. Plato's discovery thus consists in pointing out the moral significance of intense self-disrespect. This manifests itself in a two-fold way: First, it expresses itself in shame, an affective, all-encompassing mood that completely fills the subject. Second, this rage-drenched self-reproach takes on the form of an inner appeal to oneself. The act of being dissatisfied with oneself proves to the thinker that the human being has an inert, even if only obscure idea of what is appropriate, of what is just and worthy of praise. When not living up to this idea, a part of the soul, that is *thymos*, lodges an appeal. With this turn to self-refusal the adventure of independence begins. Only he who is able to disapprove of himself is able to control himself.

The sense of being bound to honor resists language, but Sloterdijk's description of *thumos* is as technical and frank a description of the combination of attunement toward purpose and energy to act that can be found. What's vital in his description is how our sense of shame forces us to action. How shame leads to self-control.

I've seen this process, of being overtaken by thumotic honor, on the battlefield. Once, on a particularly dusty and dry day in Baghdad, our patrol was led to the body of a man who had been tortured and murdered. I was acting as a Humvee gunner, sitting out of the turret and manning a 240B machine gun. With me in the vehicle was an officer, higher ranking than our platoon leader, who had yet to encounter the war dead. This was his first time, so I guess, at seeing a corpse outside of a funeral home back in America. It was incumbent upon him to get out of the vehicle and take charge. But he paused. He hesitated. The moment lasted much longer than it should have, and in that pregnant expanse of time, it seemed as though the officer went through Sloterdijk's entire process of self-shame. He was afraid and disgusted, then disgusted with himself. He let out a feeble, "Well, I suppose I should get out there…" Followed by another moment of renewed self-loathing. But somehow, in that space, he gathered the courage, the thumos, to harness his honor, leave the Humvee and walk over toward the American troops gathering around the body.

His pause felt like one of the longest moments of the war. In it was contained an epic narrative of self-reproach transforming into self-control. It was honor defining itself through action.

Postscript

You might think after reading this book that I miss being in the Army. I don't. I wasn't a very good soldier, to be honest. I think I was fine in a combat zone, but back in the barracks I was a mess. I'm not a natural runner. I can't tie knots very well. I'm not a great mechanic and I have an ambivalent relationship with authority. But all the things that I discuss in this book, the boredom, hierarchy, ritual, smoking, honor, etc. I miss all of these things. Life suffers without them, or their equivalent, present in some form. And any political program that ignores or devalues them renders itself incomplete.

Hierarchy? Authority? Honor? I'm well aware how, standing alone and without context, these terms come off as reactionary shibboleths. Especially in our "current political climate," to cop an oft-used phrase. But I don't believe any *au currant* political perspective has a monopoly on them. Re-understood, re-contextualized within a progressive, Marxist, Left Christian or even an Anarchist agenda, these terms could refer instead to the fruits of collective political action rather than dead weights. Specters from a regressive past. Perhaps the only agenda one needs in order to appreciate them is a culturally Humanist one. In other words, there's still opportunity to reject them outright for political reasons, so long as that rejection is paired with an awareness of the full scope of what's actually being dismissed.

My own goals in writing this are decidedly apolitical, a piece with the same spirit with which Charles Péguy wrote that "The revolution will be a moral revolution or it will not be a revolution at all." Of course, political claims are made in the process. A skepticism with capitalism. A questioning of materialism in its crudest forms. A longing for values which gesture toward transcendence. But I hope there's enough psychology, metaphysics, and poetics in the book (I scrupulously avoid calling it a "text") to keep it from being mistaken for a political tract. At root, this is my attempt to make sense of myself. To give my experiences form and logical coherence.

If there's any personal tragedy to this tale it's that I had to join the Army to experience these things. After coming to know their existential value first hand, our contemporary world feels doubly empty being denuded of them.

As time has passed, people ask me less and less about my intentions in joining the Army. People also thank me less for my service. It's a mixed blessing, because now I think that if someone asked me why I'd joined up I might finally be able to begin to articulate an answer.

Acknowledgments

I'd like to thank everyone I had the honor of serving with, as well as the friends and family who read portions of this book in manuscript form. Your feedback was invaluable. I would specifically like to thank Glenn Rehn, Eduardo Duarte, Tyler Malone, Jacob Silverman, Corey Kloos and Michael Schapira for their support and encouragement through the writing process.

Bibliography

Agamben, Giorgio. *The Sacrament of Language: An Archeology of the Oath*. Trans. Adam Kostko. Stanford: Stanford University Press, 2010.

Barthelme, Donald. *The Dead Father*. New York: FSG Classics, 2004.

Bly, Robert. *The Sibling Society: An Impassioned Call for the Rediscovery of Adulthood*. New York: Vintage, 1997.

Bowman, James, *Honor: A History*. New York: Encounter Books, 2007.

Boym, Svetlana, *The Future of Nostalgia*. New York: Basic Books, 2002.

Brooks, Rosa. *How Everything Became War and the Military Became Everything*. New York: Simon & Schuster, 2016.

Bunge, Gabriel. *Despondency: The Spiritual Teaching of Evagrius of Pontus*. Yonkers: St Vladimir's Seminary Press, 2011.

Cazeaux, Clive (Ed.). *The Continental Aesthetics Reader*. Abingdon: Routledge, 2011.

Châtelet, Gilles. *To Live and Think Like Pigs*. Trans. Robin Mackay. New York: Sequence Press, 2014.

Clausewitz, Carl von. *On War*. Trans. by Michael Eliot Howard and Peter Paret. Princeton: Princeton University Press, 1989.

Congar, Yves. *The Meaning of Tradition*. Trans. by A.N. Woodrow. San Francisco: Ignatius Press, 2004.

DeLillo, Don. *White Noise*. London: Penguin Press, 1999.

Douglas, Mary. *Natural Symbols: Explorations in Cosmology*. Abingdon: Routledge, 2003.

Dyer, Geoff. *The Missing of the Somme*. New York: Vintage Books, 1994.

Ellul, Jacques. *Perspectives on Our Age: Jacques Ellul Speaks on His Life and Work*. Toronto: House of Anansi Press, 1997.

Fitzgerald, F. Scott. *The Great Gatsby*. New York: Scribner, 2004.

Gaddis, William. *The Recognitions*. Champaign: Dalkey Archive Press, 2012.

Giamo, Benedict. *Kerouac, the Word and the Way: Prose Artist as Spiritual Quester*. Carbondale: Southern Illinois University Press, 2000.

Gilson, Etienne. *The Arts of the Beautiful*. Trans. James Colbert. Champaign: Dalkey Archive Press, 2007.

Gray, John. *The Silence of Animals: On Progress and Other Modern Myths*. London: Macmillan, 2013.

Han, Byung-Chul. *The Burnout Society*. trans. by Erik Butler. Stanford: Stanford University Press, 2015. *Shanzhai: Deconstruction in Chinese*, trans. by Philippa Hurd. Boston: The MIT Press, 2017. *The Scent of Time: A Philosophical Essay on the Art of Lingering*, trans. by Daniel Steuer. Cambridge: Polity, 2017.

Handleman, Don (Ed.). *Ritual in Its Own Right: Exploring the Dynamics of Transformation*. New York: Berghahn Books, 2005.

Harrison, Robert Pogue. *The Dominion of the Dead*. Chicago: University of Chicago Press, 2005.

Hauerwas, Stanley. *A Community of Character: Toward a Constructive Christian Social Ethic*. South Bend: University of Notre Dame Press, 1993.

Heidegger, Martin. *Being and Time*, Reprint edition. New York: Harper Perennial Modern Classics, 2008.

Hemingway, Ernest. *For Whom the Bell Tolls*. New York: Scribner, 1995.

Howe, Daniel Walker. *What Hath God Wrought: The Transformation of America, 1815-1848*. Oxford: Oxford University Press, 2007.

Hulliung, Mark, ed. *Rousseau and the Dilemmas of Modernity*. New Brunswick: Transaction Publishers, 2015.

Jacobson, Bernard. *Robert Motherwell: The Making of an American Giant*. London: 21 Publishing Ltd, 2015.

Jodorowsky, Alejandro. *The Way of the Tarot: The Spiritual Teacher in the Cards*. Rochester, Vermont: Destiny Books, 2009.

Jones, David. *In Parenthesis*. New York: New York Review Books Classics, 2003.

Junger, Ernst. *The Glass Bees*. Trans. Louise Bogan and Elizabeth Mayer. New York: New York Review of Books, 2000.

Junger, Sebastian. *Tribe: On Homecoming and Belonging*. New York: Grand Central Publishing, 2017.

Kaye, Sharon and Martin, Robert. *On Ockham*. Boston: Cengage Learning, 2000.

Kerouac, Jack. *On the Road*. New York: Penguin Press, 2003.

Klein, Naomi. *The Shock Doctrine: The Rise of Disaster Capitalism*. New York: Picador, 2008.

Klein, Richard. *Cigarettes Are Sublime*. Durham: Duke University Press, 1995.

Kundera, Milan. *The Unbearable Lightness of Being: A Novel*. New York: Harper Perennial Modern Classics, 2009.

Lewis, C.S. *The Four Loves*. San Francisco: HarperOne, 2017.

Lord, Albert B. *The Singer of Tales*, ed. by Stephen Mitchell and Gregory Nagy. Cambridge: Harvard University Press, 2000.

Louÿs, Pierre. *une volupté nouvelle et autres contes*. Talence: L'arbre Vengeur, 2008.

Mallarme, Stéphane. *Collected Poems*. Trans. by Henry Weinfield. Berkeley: University of California Press, 1994.

McCarthy, Cormac. *Blood Meridian*. New York: Vintage Press, 1992.

Merleau-Ponty, Maurice. *The Merleau-Ponty Reader*. Evanston: Northwestern University Press, 2007.

Mishima, Yukio. *The Sailor Who Fell from Grace with the Sea*. Trans. by John Nathan. New York: Random House, 1994.

Mumford, Lewis. *The City in History: Its Origins, Its Transformations, and Its Prospects*. London: Mariner Books, 1968.

Nault, Jean-Charles. *The Noonday Devil*. San Francisco: Ignatius Press, 2015.

Nisbet, Robert. *The Quest for Community*. Wilmington: Intercollegiate Studies Institute, 2010.

O'Brien, Tim. *The Things They Carried*. New York: Mariner Books, 2009.

Pound, Ezra. *The Cantos of Ezra Pound*, Reprint edition. New York: New Directions, 1996.

Rayner, Timothy. *Foucault's Heidegger: Philosophy and Transformative Experience*. London: Continuum, 2007.

Remarque, Erich. *All Quiet on the Western Front*. Trans. by A.W. Wheen. New York: Ballantine, 1987.

Sartre, Jean Paul. *No Exit and Three Other Plays*. Trans. by Stuart Gilbert. New York: Vintage International, 1989.

Sennett, Richard. *Authority*. New York: W.W. Norton & Company, 1993.

Skelly, Julia. *Addiction and British Visual Culture, 1751-1919: Wasted Looks*. Abingdon: Routledge, 2014.

Sloterdijk, Peter. *Rage and Time: A Psychopolitical Investigation*. trans. by Mario Wenning, Reprint edition. New York: Columbia University Press, 2012.

Somé, Malidoma Patrice. *Ritual: Power, Healing and Community*. London: Penguin Books, 2007.

Sommers, Tamler. *Why Honor Matters*. New York: Basic Books, 2018.

Stephenson, Barry. *Ritual: A Very Short Introduction*. Oxford: Oxford University Press, 2015.

Stevens, Anthony. *Archetype Revisited: An Updated Natural History of the Self*. Toronto: Inner City Books, 2003.

Stewart, Frank Henderson. *Honor*. Chicago: University of Chicago Press, 1994.

Stiegler, Bernard. *Acting Out*. Trans. David Barison. Stanford: Stanford University Press, 2009.

Tanner, Grafton, *Babbling Corpse: Vaporwave and The Commodification of Ghosts*. Winchester: Zero Books, 2016.

Taylor, Charles. *A Secular Age*. Cambridge: Harvard University Press, 2007.

Thoreau, Henry David. *Walden and Other Writings*. New York:

Modern Library, 1992.

Tocqueville, Alexis. *Democracy in America*. Trans. Harvey Mansfield. Chicago: University of Chicago Press, 2002.

Vanier, Jean. *Community and Growth*. Mahwah: Paulist Press, 1989.

Vico, Giambattista. *New Science*, trans. by Dave Marsh. London: Penguin Classics, 2000.

Voegelin, Eric. *What Is History? And Other Late Unpublished Writings*, ed. by Thomas A. Hollweck and Paul Caringella. Baton Rouge: Louisiana State University Press, 1990.

Wallace, David Foster. *Infinite Jest*. New York: Back Bay Books, 2006. *The Pale King*. New York: Little, Brown and Company, 2011.

Weil, Simone. *The Iliad or the Poem of Force*. Trans. by James P. Holoka. New York: Peter Lange   Publishing, 2006.

Biography

Scott Beauchamp is a writer who lives in Maine. His previous work has appeared in the *Paris Review Daily*, *The Atlantic Monthly*, *Bookforum* and *American Affairs*, among other places.

CULTURE, SOCIETY & POLITICS

Contemporary culture has eliminated the concept and public figure of the intellectual. A cretinous anti-intellectualism presides, cheer-led by hacks in the pay of multinational corporations who reassure their bored readers that there is no need to rouse themselves from their stupor. Zer0 Books knows that another kind of discourse – intellectual without being academic, popular without being populist – is not only possible: it is already flourishing. Zer0 is convinced that in the unthinking, blandly consensual culture in which we live, critical and engaged theoretical reflection is more important than ever before.

If you have enjoyed this book, why not tell other readers by posting a review on your preferred book site.

Recent bestsellers from Zero Books are:

In the Dust of This Planet
Horror of Philosophy vol. 1
Eugene Thacker
In the first of a series of three books on the Horror of Philosophy, *In the Dust of This Planet* offers the genre of horror as a way of thinking about the unthinkable.
Paperback: 978-1-84694-676-9 ebook: 978-1-78099-010-1

Capitalist Realism
Is there No Alternative?
Mark Fisher
An analysis of the ways in which capitalism has presented itself as the only realistic political-economic system.
Paperback: 978-1-84694-317-1 ebook: 978-1-78099-734-6

Rebel Rebel
Chris O'Leary
David Bowie: every single song. Everything you want to know, everything you didn't know.
Paperback: 978-1-78099-244-0 ebook: 978-1-78099-713-1

Cartographies of the Absolute
Alberto Toscano, Jeff Kinkle
An aesthetics of the economy for the twenty-first century.
Paperback: 978-1-78099-275-4 ebook: 978-1-78279-973-3

Malign Velocities
Accelerationism and Capitalism
Benjamin Noys
Long listed for the Bread and Roses Prize 2015, *Malign Velocities* argues against the need for speed, tracking acceleration as the symptom of the ongoing crises of capitalism.
Paperback: 978-1-78279-300-7 ebook: 978-1-78279-299-4

Meat Market
Female Flesh under Capitalism
Laurie Penny
A feminist dissection of women's bodies as the fleshy fulcrum of capitalist cannibalism, whereby women are both consumers and consumed.
Paperback: 978-1-84694-521-2 ebook: 978-1-84694-782-7

Poor but Sexy
Culture Clashes in Europe East and West
Agata Pyzik
How the East stayed East and the West stayed West.
Paperback: 978-1-78099-394-2 ebook: 978-1-78099-395-9

Romeo and Juliet in Palestine
Teaching Under Occupation
Tom Sperlinger
Life in the West Bank, the nature of pedagogy and the role of a
university under occupation.
Paperback: 978-1-78279-637-4 ebook: 978-1-78279-636-7

Sweetening the Pill
or How We Got Hooked on Hormonal Birth Control
Holly Grigg-Spall
Has contraception liberated or oppressed women? *Sweetening
the Pill* breaks the silence on the dark side of hormonal
contraception.
Paperback: 978-1-78099-607-3 ebook: 978-1-78099-608-0

Why Are We The Good Guys?
Reclaiming your Mind from the Delusions of Propaganda
David Cromwell
A provocative challenge to the standard ideology that Western
power is a benevolent force in the world.
Paperback: 978-1-78099-365-2 ebook: 978-1-78099-366-9

Readers of ebooks can buy or view any of these bestsellers by
clicking on the live link in the title. Most titles are published
in paperback and as an ebook. Paperbacks are available in
traditional bookshops. Both print and ebook formats are available
online.
Find more titles and sign up to our readers' newsletter
at http://www.johnhuntpublishing.com/culture-and-politics
Follow us on Facebook
at https://www.facebook.com/ZeroBooks
and Twitter at https://twitter.com/Zer0Books